Fiqh Ma

A Basic Textbook on Fiqh

By
Dr. Saalih ibn Ghaanim al-Sadlaan
Professor, College of Shareeah
Muhammad ibn Saud Islamic University
Riyadh, Saudi Arabia

Translated by
Jamaal al-Din M. Zarabozo

تيسير الفقه

بقلم الأستاذ الدكتور صالح بن غانم السدلان

نقله إلى الإنجليزية جمال الدين زربوزو

Fiqh Made Easy: A Basic Textbook on Fiqh
By Dr. Saalih Ghaanim al-Sadlaan
Translated by Jamaal al-Din M. Zarabozo

Published by:

Al-Basheer Company for Publications and Translations
3700 Havana St. Suite 102
Denver, CO 80239
U.S.A.
303-574-0095 fax: 303-373-0943
www.al-basheer.com

(Note: Not affiliated with Basheer Publications)

ISBN 1-891540-07-6 $11.00 softcover

Table of Contents

TRANSLATOR'S INTRODUCTION 1

INTRODUCTION 5

PART ONE: ACTS OF WORSHIP 9

CHAPTER ONE: PURITY 11

INTRODUCTION 11
   Definition *11*
   The Different Types...*11*
TOPIC ONE: A DISCUSSION OF WATER 12
   (1) Water That Is Purifying...*12*
   (2) Water That Is Pure [But Which Cannot Be Used As A
   Purifying Agent] *13*
   (3) Impure Water *13*
   Related Points..*13*
TOPIC TWO: CONTAINERS AND UTENSILS 14
   Definition...*14*
   The Different Types of Containers and Utensils....................*14*
   The Islamic Ruling Concerning Utensils *15*
   The Containers and Utensils of Non-Muslims *15*
   Related Points..*16*
TOPIC THREE: IMPURITIES AND THEIR RULINGS....................16
   Definition...*16*
   The Types of Impurities...*17*
   The Categories of Impurities *17*
   (1) Agreed Upon Impurities..*17*
   (2) Impurities Concerning Which There is
   Some Disagreement *18*
   (3) Impurities Pardoned by the Shareeah..............................*18*

The Manner of Purifying [or Removing] Impurities.................19

TOPIC FOUR: ETIQUETTE AND CLEANING ONESELF AFTER
RELIEVING ONESELF...19

TOPIC FIVE: THE ACTS CORRESPONDING TO THE NATURE OF
HUMANS (SUNAN AL-FITRA) 21
    Definition...21
    The Sunan al-Fitra ((سنن الفطرة))...21

TOPIC SIX: ABLUTION (WUDHU)..22
    Definition of al-Wudhu ((الوضوء)...22
    The Virtues of Wudhu 23
    The Prerequisites for the Wudhu 24
    Actions That Obligate the Making of Ablution 24
    The Obligatory Acts of the Ablution 25
    The Recommended Acts of the Ablution 25
    Disliked Acts Related to the Ablution 26
    What Nullifies One's Ablution 27

TOPIC SEVEN: GHUSL OR COMPLETE WASHING............................27
    The Lexical and Technical Definition of Ghusl 27
    The Acts That Obligate Ghusl..28
    Acts For Which Ghusl is Recommended.......................................28
    The Prerequisites of the Ghusl..29
    The Mandatory Acts of the Ghusl 29
    The Obligatory Acts of the Ghusl 29
    The Recommended Acts of the Ghusl...30
    Disliked Acts Related to the Ghusl..30
    Acts Forbidden for the Person Required to Make Ghusl..........30

TOPIC EIGHT: TAYAMMUM...31
    Lexical and Technical Definition...31
    Who is Allowed to Resort to Tayammum 31
    Prerequisites for the Obligation of Tayammum...........................31
    Conditions for the Soundness of the Tayammum.........................32
    The Obligatory Portions of the Tayammum..................................32
    The Recommended Portions of the Tayammum.............................32
    What Negates the Tayammum..32
    The Manner in Which Tayammum is Performed 33
    Tayammum for Casts and Injuries...33

TOPIC NINE: WIPING OVER LEATHER SANDALS, [SOCKS] OR
SPLINTS 33

CHAPTER TWO: THE PRAYER (*AL-SALAAT*)........................35

INTRODUCTION 35
Lexical and Technical Definition.....................................35
Its Obligatory Nature...36
The Wisdom Behind Its Legislation 36
TOPIC ONE: SOME REGULATIONS RELATED TO PRAYER 37
The Ruling Concerning the Prayer and The
Number of Prayers...37
Ordering the Young to Pray 39
The Ruling Concerning One Who Denies the Obligation of
Prayer 39
The Essential Components (Arkaan) of the Prayer 40
The Obligatory Acts (Waajibaat) of the Prayer...............41
The Prerequisites for the Prayer......................................42
The Timings for the Five Daily Prayers............................42
The Timings for the Prayers in Very Northern or Southern
Lands 44
TOPIC TWO: CONGREGATIONAL PRAYER 46
Wisdom Behind Its Legislation 46
The Ruling Concerning Congregational Prayer................46
What Constitutes a Congregational Prayer.......................47
The Place Where the Congregational Prayer is to Be Held.....47
TOPIC THREE: SHORTENING AND COMBINING PRAYERS 48
The Meaning of Shortening the Prayers 48
Shortening the Prayers Generally, While in a State of Security
or Otherwise 48
The Distance That Allows One to Shorten the Prayer While
Traveling...49
When One Begins to Shorten the Prayer 49
Combining the Prayers 49
Combining at the Earlier or the Later Time 50
[TOPIC:] THE PROSTRATIONS OF FORGETFULNESS 50
TOPIC FOUR: VOLUNTARY PRAYERS 51

The Wisdom Behind Their Legislation.................................51
The Best Voluntary Acts...51
Some of the Voluntary Prayers:.......................................52
The Late-Night Prayers 52
The Dhuha Prayer 52
The Prayer for "Greeting" the Mosque...............................53
Prostration While Reading [Specific Verses] of the Quran......53
Prostration of Thankfulness...54
The Taraweeh Prayer 54
The Witr Prayer..55
The Regular [Daily] Sunnah Prayers 55
TOPIC FIVE: THE FRIDAY PRAYER.......................................56
The Virtue of Friday 56
The Status of the Friday Prayer.......................................57
Upon Whom is the Friday Prayer Obligatory 57
The Timing for the Friday Prayer.....................................57
What Number Can Constitute the Friday Prayer 57
Conditions for the Validity of the Friday Prayer...................58
TOPIC SIX: THE EID PRAYERS...58
The Wisdom Behind Their Legislation...............................58
Its Status 59
Its Conditions..59
Its Timing...59
How the Eid Prayer is Performed.....................................59
The Place in Which It is to Be Prayed...............................60
Recommended Acts Related to the Eid Prayers....................60
TOPIC SEVEN: THE PRAYER FOR RAIN (AL-ISTISQAA) AND THE
ECLIPSE PRAYERS (AL-KUSOOF) 61
The Prayer for Rain:..61
The Wisdom Behind Its Legislation 61
Its Meaning...62
Its Status 62
The Prayer of the Eclipse (al-Kusoof):..............................62
The Meaning of al-Kusoof and the Wisdom Behind
the Prayer 62
TOPIC EIGHT: THE FUNERAL PRAYER 64

Washing the Deceased 65

Description of the Recommended Way to Wash the Deceased . 65

Shrouding the Deceased 66

Description of the Prayer Over the Deceased 66

The Virtue of Praying the Prayer Over the Deceased 70

*Description of the Grave and Burial and What is
Prohibited at the Gravesites* 70

CHAPTER THREE: *ZAKAAT* **73**

INTRODUCTION 73

The Wisdom of Legislating Zakaat 73

The Definition of Zakaat 73

The Place of Zakaat in Islam 74

The Status of Zakaat 74

TOPIC ONE: SOME RULES CONCERNING *ZAKAAT* 75

The Types of Wealth Upon Which Zakaat is Obligatory 75

*(1) The Zakaat on Monetary Assets: Gold, Silver
and Currency* 76

(2) The Zakaat on Livestock 76

Zakaat on Agricultural Produce 78

What is Obligatory Concerning Grains and Produce 78

Zakaat on Merchandise Goods 79

The Conditions for the Obligation of Zakaat 79

Paying the Zakaat: 80

The Time for Paying the Zakaat 80

The Ruling Concerning Withholding Zakaat 80

Recommended Acts When Paying Zakaat 81

The Recipients of Zakaat 81

TOPIC TWO: ZAKAAT AL-FITR 82

Its Wisdom 82

*Its Amount and the Types of Foods in Which it is to
Be Given* 83

The Time of Its Obligation and the Time of Its Payment 83

Upon Whom is Zakaat al-Fitr Obligatory 83

The Recipients of Zakaat al-Fitr 84

CHAPTER FOUR: THE FAST 85

INTRODUCTION 85
Definition of Fasting.................................85
The History of the Obligation of Fasting...............85
The Benefits of Fasting 86
Confirming the Beginning of the Month of Ramadhaan...........86
The Obligation of Fasting Ramadhaan 88
TOPIC ONE: CONDITIONS RELATED TO FASTING 89
The Conditions Requiring One to Fast..................89
The Essential Components of the Fast..................89
The Conditions for the Soundness of the Fast 89
Recommended Acts of the Fast 90
Actions That are Disliked During the Fast.............91
TOPIC TWO: ACCEPTABLE EXCUSES TO NOT FAST...........91
What Nullifies the Fast 92
Important Notes 92
TOPIC FOUR: *ITIKAAF*...................................93
Definition..93
The Wisdom Behind Its Being Sanctioned 94
The Types of Itikaaf 94
The Essential Components of Itikaaf 94
The Conditions for the Soundness of the Itikaaf.......95
The Itikaaf is Voided by the Following Acts 95
Excuses That Permit One to Leave the Mosque...........95

CHAPTER FIVE: HAJJ [PILGRIMAGE] AND UMRAH [LESSER VISITATION] 97

INTRODUCTION 97
The Place of the Pilgrimage in Islam 97
The Legal Status of the Pilgrimage....................98
The Umrah [Lesser Visitation] 99
The Wisdom Behind the Enjoining of Hajj and Umrah.....99
TOPIC ONE: THE CONDITIONS OF THE HAJJ AND UMRAH 99
The Conditions of Obligation 99
The Different Ways in Which the Pilgrimage

Can Be Performed 100
TOPIC THREE: THE ESSENTIAL COMPONENTS OF THE HAJJ AND
UMRAH 101
The First Essential 102
The Obligatory Aspects of the Inviolable State.....................102
The Second Essential: The Circumambulation......................103
Recommended Aspects for the Circumambulation 104
The Third Essential: The Sa'ee...105
The Conditions of the Sa'ee..105
The Recommended Acts of the Sa'ee 106
The Fourth Essential: Stopping at Arafah.............................107
TOPIC THREE: THE OBLIGATORY ACTS OF THE HAJJ AND UMRAH107
The Obligatory Acts of the Hajj...107
The Obligatory Acts of the Umrah...108
Important Notes 108
TOPIC FOUR: ACTS FORBIDDEN FOR ONE IN THE INVIOLABLE
STATE 108
TOPIC FIVE: THE SPECIFIC TIMES AND LOCATIONS FOR ENTERING
INTO THE INVIOLABLE STATE 112
TOPIC SIX: THE SACRIFICE AND AQEEQAH................................114
The Sacrifice 114
The Timing of the Sacrifice...114
The Aqeeqah 115

CHAPTER SIX: JIHAD 117
Definition 117
The Wisdom Behind Its Legislation 117
The Legal Status of the Jihad...117
The Conditions for Jihad to Be Obligatory............................118
The Different Types of Jihad...118
The Virtues with Allah Awaiting the Martyr..........................119
Etiquette of War..119
The Captives of War 119
How the Army Should Treat Their Leader..............................120

PART TWO: TRANSACTIONS AMONG HUMANS 121

CHAPTER ONE: BUSINESS TRANSACTIONS **123**

INTRODUCTION 123
Lexical and Legal Definition of Bai' 123
The Wisdom Behind Legalizing Buying and Selling 123
TOPIC ONE: THE ESSENTIAL COMPONENTS AND CONDITIONS FOR
BUYING AND SELLING 124
The Essential Components of Buying and Selling 124
The Form of the Transaction 124
Transactions Over the Phone 125
The Conditions for a Sound Business Transaction 125
Stipulations in the Contract 126
TOPIC TWO: PROHIBITED TRANSACTIONS 127

CHAPTER TWO: *RIBA* (INTEREST) AND ITS RULINGS....129

INTRODUCTION 129
The Definition of Riba 129
The Wisdom Behind the Prohibition of Riba 129
TOPIC ONE: THE TYPES OF *RIBA* 130
TOPIC TWO: THE DOORS THAT ISLAM OPENS TO FREEDOM FROM
RIBA 132
TOPIC THREE: INTEREST PAID BY BANKS 133

CHAPTER THREE: LEASING, RENTING AND HIRING.....135

INTRODUCTION 135
Definition of Ijaarah (Leasing, Renting or Hiring) 135
Its Legal Status 135
The Wisdom Behind Its Sanctioning 135
Two Types of Ijaarah 136
TOPIC ONE: CONDITIONS REQUIRED FOR LEASING AND WHAT IS
BEING HIRED OR LEASED 136
The Conditions for Leasing 136
Conditions for What is Being Leased or Hired 137
TOPIC TWO: ISSUES RELATED TO *IJAARAH* 137

CHAPTER FOUR: ENDOWMENTS..**139**

INTRODUCTION 139
  Lexical and Legal Definition of an Endowment *139*
  The Basis for the Legality of Endowments..........................*139*
  The Wisdom Behind Sanctioning Endowments......................*140*
  The Wording of the Endowment.......................................*141*
TOPIC ONE: THE TYPES OF ENDOWMENTS AND WHAT MAY BE
GIVEN AS ENDOWMENTS 142
  Types of Endowments *142*
  What is Proper to Be Made Endowments *142*
TOPIC TWO: THE CONDITIONS FOR AN ENDOWMENT 143
  Conditions for the One Making the Endowment.....................*143*
  Conditions for What is Being Made an Endowment...............*144*
  How to Use the Benefits of Endowments *145*
TOPIC THREE: THE DIFFERENCE BETWEEN AN ENDOWMENT
AND A BEQUEST 145

CHAPTER FIVE: BEQUESTS **147**

INTRODUCTION 147
  Definition of a Bequest *147*
  The Basis for the Legality of a Bequest *147*
  What Constitutes the Making of a Bequest *148*
TOPIC ONE: THE TYPES OF BEQUESTS AND ITS LEGAL STATUS ..149
  The Legal Status of a Bequest...*149*
  The Types of Bequests..*149*
  The Amount of a Bequest *150*
  What is Taken Into Consideration for the
  Bequest to Be Valid...*150*
TOPIC TWO: THE CONDITIONS OF A BEQUEST 151
  Conditions for the One Making the Bequest..........................*151*
  Conditions for the One for Whom the Bequest is Made..........*151*
  Conditions for What is Being Bequeathed...........................*152*
  Confirming a Bequest *152*
  The Types of Executors *152*
TOPIC THREE: NULLIFIERS OF THE BEQUEST 153

PART THREE: FAMILY MATTERS **155**

CHAPTER ONE: MARRIAGE AND ITS RULINGS 157

INTRODUCTION 157
The Wisdom for Legalizing Marriage.................................*157*
The Wisdom Behind Marriage..*158*
Lexical and Legal Definition of Marriage............................*158*
TOPIC ONE: CONDITIONS FOR MARRIAGE AND
ITS LEGAL STATUS 159
The Legal Status of Marriage..*159*
Its Verbal Form..*159*
The Essential Components of a Marriage Contract..............*159*
The Conditions for a Marriage Contract..............................*160*
TOPIC TWO: WHAT IS RECOMMENDED AND WHAT IS FORBIDDEN
WITH REGARDS TO MARRIAGE 161

CHAPTER TWO: RULINGS PARTICULAR FOR MUSLIM
WOMEN..163

INTRODUCTION 163
ISSUES SPECIFICALLY RELATED TO WOMEN 163
The First Issue: Wiping Over a Wig.....................................*163*
The Second Issue: Fingernail or Toenail Polish....................*164*
The Third Issue: Menstruation...*164*
The Fourth Issue: Post-Partum Bleeding..............................*165*
*The Fifth Issue: al-Istahaadhah (Abnormal Prolonged
Flow of Blood)*...*165*
The Sixth Issue: Shaving Hair and Other Issues...................*166*
The Seventh Issue: The Aurah of a Woman............................*166*
The Eighth Issue: Beautification for Women..........................*167*
The Ninth Issue: The Voice of Women....................................*167*
The Tenth Issue: Related to Death and Funerals...................*168*
The Eleventh Issue: Jewelry...*168*
The Twelfth Issue: Women Giving Charity.............................*168*
The Thirteenth Issue: Breaking the Fast...............................*169*
The Fourteenth Issue: Performing the Pilgrimage................*169*
The Fifteenth Issue: Clothing During the Pilgrimage...........*170*

The Sixteenth Issue: Pilgrimage During Menses and Post-Partum Bleeding *170*

The Seventeenth Issue: The Talbiyyah *170*

The Eighteenth Issue: Cutting the Hair as a Rite of Pilgrimage *170*

The Nineteenth Issue: The Farewell Circumam-bulation *171*

The Twentieth Issue: Marrying Non-Muslims *171*

The Twenty-First Issue: Custody *172*

The Twenty-Second Issue: Covering the Face *172*

Translator's Introduction

In the name of Allah, Most Compassionate, Most Merciful. All praises are due to Allah; we praise Him; we seek His help; we seek His forgiveness; and we seek His guidance. We seek refuge in Allah from the evil in our souls and the badness of our deeds. For whomever Allah guides, there is none to lead him astray. And for whomever He allows to go astray, there is none to guide him. I bear witness that there is none worthy of worship except Allah, for whom there is no partner. And I bear witness that Muhammad is His servant and Messenger.

In this work, the author has done an excellent job of concisely mentioning the most important aspects of the different fiqh topics he discussed. Furthermore, he has discussed many issues that are not greatly discussed in the English literature, such as the rules concerning bequests and endowments. Hence, this work was chosen to be translated as a welcomed addition to the available English literature.

It should be noted that this work was first written with the intention that it would be translated as a basic and introductory work on fiqh for the Islamic republics that formerly formed part of the U.S.S.R. To meet that goal, the author was forced to keep this book free of details and arguments over different fiqh opinions. Therefore, he had the unenviable task of presenting his conclusions without stating his evidence or reasoning.

For the greater portion of this book, the fiqh opinions expressed are generally agreed upon and non-controversial. Obviously, there are going to be some other points concerning which there is difference of opinion. On these points, many of Dr. al-Sadlaan's conclusions may be criticized or questioned by some readers. (Some readers may even note that in this translator's own writings, he disagrees with the author on various points.) One may even come across some points that seem very odd or unheard of. However, one must keep in mind that Dr. Saalih al-Sadlaan is one of the most well-read scholars today and he has never obliged himself to follow a particular *madhhab* (school of fiqh). Hence, at the very least, the views expressed in this work are the conclusions of a well-respected scholar who a specialist in the field of fiqh. Furthermore, upon study, one can find that all of the views mentioned by Dr. al-Sadlaan in this work are held by at least one or more of the famous scholars in the history of Islam. Again, due to the nature of this work, he does not mention which of the famous scholars held these same opinions. Furthermore, he does not state why he felt that such was the strongest or correct opinion. But that is the nature of this type of work. If the author had gone into those details, it would have defeated the purpose of the work.

Due to the points made above, much debate was held over whether or not a work of this nature needs to or should be published at this time, even though the disputed points are actually relatively small in number. It was finally concluded that the book should be published as its publication would entail many benefits. First, it was decided that it may be very good to expose people to different fiqh opinions. Knowledge and awareness is a definite key in avoiding some of the disputes— and even hatred— that are occurring among Muslims. There is a disturbing trend among some Muslims today to think that their fiqh opinion is the only opinion and no other opinion has any worth to it whatsoever. Other opinions are sometimes even ridiculed and not tolerated in any way. In reality, though, there may be many other opinions that have some evidence for them— even though one may conclude that they are weaker opinions.[1] Furthermore, there are well-known scholars who have come to those conclusions. Hence, those opinions are worthy of some respect and of understanding between the people who hold different opinions. This is a very important point as people are going to differ on fiqh matters. Allah, in His wisdom, did not make every fiqh issue definitive with no room for scholarly judgment and reasoning. This is an undeniable fact and, therefore, one has to accept that others may come to different conclusions. The result of these differences of opinion should not be division and hatred. There has to be some room for tolerance and discussion. In fact, through discussion and exploration one often finds that what he believed to be the strongest opinion without doubt turns out to be the weaker opinion.

Second, it was decided to publish this book because it can be excellent as a textbook for workshops and schools, as well as a primer for new Muslims. There is definitely a need for such books in English. The fundamental, agreed upon points are presented clearly for the teacher and the students. Teachers and Imams may expound on the evidence for the positions that Dr. al-Sadlaan holds and discuss the issues in greater detail. Hence, it may lay the foundation for a much better understanding of the essential topics that Dr. al-Sadlaan has chosen to discuss in this introductory work.

Throughout the translation, this translator has kept his comments to a minimum. At times, though, one will find words added to the text in brackets; this was only resorted to when it was felt that the text in itself may still be unclear to some readers or if something was obviously inadvertently left out by the author.

Finally, thanks must be expressed to Shaikh Dr. Saalih al-Sadlaan for his kind permission to translate this work that

---

[1] The causes of differences of opinion, acceptable and non-acceptable differences, and how to deal with differences in opinion will be dealt with by this author in a future work, Allah willing.

he prepared for a very noble cause. May Allah reward him handsomely. Thanks and appreciation must also go to Sr. Imaan for her editing and proofreading of the work. And, last but not least, thinks must also be extended to my wife for her efforts and proofreading of the work. May Allah grant them all Paradise.

Jamaal Zarabozo
Boulder, CO
Dec. 1, 1999

Introduction

Verily, all praises are to Allah; we praise Him, seek His help and seek His guidance. We seek refuge in Him from the evil of our souls and the sinfulness of our deeds. Whomever Allah guides, there is none to lead astray; and whomever He lets stray, there is none who can guide him. I bear witness that there is none worthy of worship except Allah, alone, who has no partners. And I bear witness that Muhammad is His servant and messenger.

يَاأَيُّهَا الَّذِينَ آمَنُوا اتَّقُوا اللَّهَ وَقُولُوا قَوْلاً سَدِيدًا يُصْلِحْ لَكُمْ أَعْمَالَكُمْ وَيَغْفِرْ لَكُمْ ذُنُوبَكُمْ وَمَنْ يُطِعْ اللَّهَ وَرَسُولَهُ فَقَدْ فَازَ فَوْزًا عَظِيمًا

"O you who believe! fear Allah, and (always) say a word directed to what is right that He may make your conduct whole and sound and forgive you your sins: he who obeys Allah and His Messenger attains the highest achievement" (*al-Ahzaab* 70-71).

May the blessings and peace of Allah be upon our leader Muhammad, His servant and Messenger, he who was sent by his Lord with guidance and the true religion so that it may prevail over all religions. By him, the blessing was completed and he was made pleased by Islam as a way of life.

To proceed:

In the religion of Islam, fiqh (Islamic jurisprudence) is the scale for the deeds of a person, with respect to determining them to be permissible, forbidden, sound or non-valid. By his nature, a Muslim is eager to know what is permissible and what is forbidden as well as what is sound or not sound from his deeds. This is true, regardless if the deed is concerning his relation with his Lord or if it is with respect to his interaction with others. The laws for such are found in the science of fiqh. This science emanates fundamentally from adhering to the clear texts of the Book of Allah and the sunnah of His Messenger as well as in the derivation of further laws from those two sources, and by the supporting of its principles and fundamentals. These principles and fundamentals have a very strong connection with the principles of ethics and behavior— all of that without the influence of desires or personal whims— in accord with the basic logic that seeks to know what Allah wants from us and orders us to do and what Allah has prohibited us from doing. [The result of that fiqh is] the distinguishing features of the excellence of the laws and principles of Islam being made clear, with respect to their comprehensiveness, flexibility and profoundness.

وَمَا كَانَ الْمُؤْمِنُونَ لِيَنفِرُوا كَافَّةً فَلَوْلَا نَفَرَ مِنْ كُلِّ فِرْقَةٍ مِنْهُمْ طَائِفَةٌ لِيَتَفَقَّهُوا فِي الدِّينِ وَلِيُنذِرُوا قَوْمَهُمْ إِذَا رَجَعُوا إِلَيْهِمْ لَعَلَّهُمْ يَحْذَرُونَ

"Nor should the believers all go forth together: if a contingent from every expedition remained behind, they could devote themselves to studies in religion, and admonish the people when they return to them, that thus they (may learn) to guard themselves (against evil)" (*al-Taubah* 122).

Studying and understanding the religion is one of the greatest ways to get closer to Allah. Similarly, spreading the laws of the Shareeah is also one of the greatest ways to get closer to Allah, especially those matters related to fiqh, so that the people may be following clear guidance with respect to their acts of worship and worldly matters which form the basis of their well-being in both this life and the Hereafter. The Messenger of Allah (peace and blessing of Allah be upon him) said,[1] "For whomever Allah desires good, He gives him an understanding of the religion."[2] "Verily, knowledge is only through learning."[3] "Certainly, the prophets— may Allah's blessings and peace be upon them— did not leave behind gold or silver coins; they only left behind knowledge. Whoever takes it, takes abundant good."[4]

This book comprises the topics that are of concern to Muslims who live in non-Arab societies. It covers the fiqh topics that are in accord with the clear statements of the Book of Allah, authentic sunnah and what the Muslim scholars and nation have agreed to. It remains away from the differences of opinion among the schools of fiqh as well as the differences concerning detailed issues that are only of interest to specialized researchers. All of this has been presented in an easy-to-understand language so that it may reach the reader in a fresh way. In that way, it will be an incentive for him to try to increase his understanding and turn more towards knowledge.

This research is comprised of three main parts as follows: part one concerns acts of worship; part two discusses interpersonal transactions; part three deals with matters related to the family.

---

[1] This translator could not find the following entire statement recorded as one hadith of the Prophet (peace be upon him). It seems, Allah knows best, that the author has combined a number of different hadith into one statement. Hence, each portion of his quote will be dealt with separately in the forthcoming footnotes.— JZ

[2] The words in this portion of the above quote were recorded by al-Bukhari and Muslim.—JZ

[3] There is a slight mistake in the wording of the printed text of al-Sadlaan's work. The translation above is based on the correct wording from *Sahih al-Bukhari*. These words were recorded by al-Bukhari in *mualaq* form (that is, without its complete chain). According to al-Albaani, it is recorded by al-Daaraqutni in *al-Afraad* and by al-Khateeb al-Baghdaadi in *Tareekh Baghdaad*. Al-Albaani has graded it to be *hasan*. See Muhammad Naasir al-Deen al-Albaani, *Saheeh al-Jaami al-Sagheer* (Beirut: al-Maktab al-Islaami, 1986), vol. 1, p. 461.—JZ

[4] Recorded by Ahmad, al-Tirmidhi, Abu Dawood, ibn Maajah and al-Daarimi. According to al-Albaani, it is *sahih*. See al-Albaani, *Saheeh al-Jaami*, vol. 2, p. 1079.—JZ

We ask Allah alone to make this deed purely for the sake of His Noble countenance. We also ask that He make this work beneficial for our Muslim brothers everywhere. He is all-Hearing, responding [to the prayers]. He is sufficient for us and the best of guardians.

Hoping for the forgiveness of his Lord

Saalih ibn Ghaanim al-Sadlaan
1st of Rajab 1415 A.H.

Part One: Acts of Worship

This part shall be comprised of the following chapters:
Chapter One: Purity
Chapter Two: Prayer
Chapter Three: Zakaat
Chapter Four: Fasting
Chapter Five: Pilgrimage
Chapter Six: Jihad

Dr. Saalih al-Sadlaan

Chapter One: Purity

This chapter shall consist of an introduction followed by the discussion of nine topics:
Topic 1: Water;
Topic 2: Vessels and Bowls;
Topic 3: Impurities;
Topic 4: Cleaning Oneself and Etiquette Related to Relieving Oneself;
Topic 5: The Acts in Accord with Human Nature;
Topic 6: Ablution (*Wudhu*);
Topic 7: *Ghusl;*
Topic 8: *Tayammum;*
Topic 9: Wiping over Shoes and Splints.

Introduction

Definition

Lexically, the word *tahaarah* (طــهارة) means cleanliness and purity. As a technical term, it means the removal of the attribute of one's body that prevents one from being allowed to pray and so forth.

The Different Types

In Islamic law, *tahaarah* has both a spiritual and a physical sense to it. The physical sense is related to the human body. The spiritual sense is the purifying of the heart from the filth of sins. The physical sense is the one related to the science of fiqh that is required for the prayer; that is, it is related to the external aspects.

The external acts of purification are of two varieties: (1) Purification after the acts that nullify one's state of purity; (2) Purification from impure substances.

Purification from the acts that nullify one's state of purity is further subdivided into three categories: (1) the major act, which is a complete washing of one's body or *ghusl* (غسل); (2) the minor act, which is ablution or *wudhu* (وضوء); and (3) the substitute for either (1) or (2) when they cannot be performed, which is known as *tayammum* (تيمم).

Purification from impure substances involves three types of acts: (1) washing, (2) wiping and (3) moistening or sprinkling.

Topic One:
A Discussion of Water

Water can be divided into the following three categories:

(1) Water That Is Purifying

Water that can be used as a means of purification is water that retains its natural characteristics [that is, free of any impurities or any change in its qualities, as described in the following categories]. This is the water that [is to be used to] remove the state of impurity or to remove any impurities that are present in an [otherwise] pure place. Allah says,

وَيُنَزِّلُ عَلَيْكُمْ مِنَ السَّمَاءِ مَاءً لِيُطَهِّرَكُمْ بِهِ

"He caused rain to descend on you from heaven, to purify yourselves therewith" (*al-Anfaal* 11).

(2) Water That Is Pure [But Which Cannot Be Used As A Purifying Agent]

Pure water is that which has had its color, taste or smell changed by a substance which is not impure. The water is pure in itself [meaning, for example, if it gets on a person's clothing, he does not have to remove it in order to pray]. However, it cannot be used as a means of purification since at least one of its characteristics has changed.

(3) Impure Water

Impure water is any water that has had one of its characteristics [of color, smell or taste] altered by something impure, whether it be a small or large amount.

Related Points

- Impure water is purified by it changing its characteristics naturally or by cleaning it or by adding enough pure water to it that the alteration is removed.
- If a Muslim is in doubt about whether some water is impure or pure, he acts on the basis of what was known for certainty: the general ruling for anything is that of purity [in other words, something is considered pure unless there is clear evidence demonstrating that it has been made impure].
- If one cannot differentiate liquid that is pure from that which is not, one leaves them both and performs *tayammum*.

- If a person is confused about garments, not knowing which is impure or forbidden from that which is pure, he bases his act on what he knows for certain and prays one prayer only [in that garment; in other words, he uses the garment he believes to be pure and prays once; he does not have to pray, change his clothing and then pray another prayer just to make sure that he prayed in a garment that was not impure or forbidden].

Topic Two:
Containers and Utensils

Definition

The word *al-aaniyah* (الآنية) is the plural of *inaa* (إناء). Lexically, it is any container or utensil used for food or drink. The legal definition of the word is the same.

The Different Types of Containers and Utensils

With respect to the composition of utensils, they can be divided into the following categories: (1) utensils made of gold or silver; (2) silver plated utensils; (3) gold plated utensils; (4) expensive utensils due to their material or way of being made; (5) leather utensils; (6) utensils made out of bone; and (7) any other type of utensils, such as those made of pottery or wood.

The Islamic Ruling Concerning Utensils

Every container or utensil made of a pure substance, costly or not costly, is permissible to be owned and used except for that made from gold or silver or plated with either of them. Hudhaifah narrated that the Prophet (peace be upon him) said,

لَا تَشْرَبُوا فِي آنِيَةِ الذَّهَبِ وَالْفِضَّةِ وَلَا تَأْكُلُوا فِي صِحَافِهَا
فَإِنَّهَا لَهُمْ فِي الدُّنْيَا وَلَنَا فِي الآخِرَة

"Do not drink from a gold or silver container and do not eat from such plates for they are for them [the disbelievers] in this world and for us [the believers] in the Hereafter." (Recorded by al-Bukhari and Muslim.)

What is forbidden to use is also forbidden to possess in a form that is to be used, like possessing musical instruments which is also forbidden.

Note that the above prohibition applies to both men and women due to the generality of the text.

Nothing is to be considered impure simply based on conjecture until one is certain that it is impure. That is, the basic or general ruling is that of purity.

The Containers and Utensils of Non-Muslims

This includes the utensils of the People of the Book [Jews and Christians] and the utensils of the polytheists. The ruling concerning these utensils is that they are permissible for use as long as one is not certain that they are impure. This is because the general ruling is that of purity.

Related Points

- The clothing of non-Muslims is considered pure as long as one is not certain that they contain some impurity.
- The skin of a dead animal from the types of animals that one is normally allowed to eat is purified by tanning.
- What is cut off from a live animal [meaning, flesh or bones] is considered impure like carrion. However, the wool, feathers, hairs and fur are considered pure even if taken from a live animal.
- It is recommended (sunnah) to cover the containers and drinking utensils and to close the mouths of waterskins. The Prophet (peace be upon him) said,

$$أَوْكِ سِقَاءَكَ وَاذْكُرِ اسْمَ اللَّهِ وَخَمِّرْ إِنَاءَكَ وَاذْكُرِ اسْمَ اللَّهِ وَلَوْ تَعْرُضُ عَلَيْهِ عودا$$

"Tie and close the mouths of the water containers and mention the name of Allah [over them]. Cover your containers, even if just with a piece of wood, and mention the name of Allah [over them]." (Recorded by al-Bukhari and Muslim.)

Topic Three:

Impurities and Their Rulings

Definition

Lexically, impurities or *al-najaasah* (النجاسة) means something filthy. Something becomes impure when it is tarnished by something filthy.

In the terminology of Islamic law, impurity refers to a specific amount of particular substances, such as urine, blood and alcohol, whose presence prohibits one from being able to perform the prayer.

The Types of Impurities

There are two types of impurities. One is something that is impure due to its essence and the second is impure with respect to its ruling. The first category includes those articles that are impure in and of themselves such that they cannot be made pure, such as dogs and pigs. The second category covers those things that are impure due to an impure substance coming upon something otherwise pure.

The Categories of Impurities

Impurities can be divided into three categories: (1) those substances concerning which there is agreement that they are impure; (2) those substances concerning which there is a disagreement that they are impure; and (3) those substances that are pardoned or overlooked by Islamic law.

(1) Agreed Upon Impurities

(1) Carrion of all land animals [except for locusts]. Dead sea animals are considered pure and permissible to eat.

(2) Blood that has been poured forth, that is, the blood that pours forth from a land animal when it is slaughtered.

(3) Pig flesh [and other parts of the pig].

(4) Human urine.

(5) Human feces.

(6) Seminal fluid.

(7) *Al-wadi* [an uncommon white substance that flows from the male private part due to a medical condition].

(8) Meat from an animal that one is not allowed to consume.

(9) [Flesh or bones] cut off from a live animal. For example, if one were to cut off the foreleg of a live sheep, that foreleg would be considered impure.

(10) Menstrual blood.

(11) Post-partum blood.

(12) Blood from a prolonged flow from the woman's private part.

[(13) *Al-madhi* or prostatic fluid which is a fluid that flows out of the sexual parts due to sexual stimulation.[1]]

(2) Impurities Concerning Which There is Some Disagreement

(1) The urine of an animal that one is permitted to eat.

(2) The feces of an animal that one is permitted to eat.

(3) Sperm.

(4) Dog's saliva.

(5) Vomit.

(6) Dead animals that do not have flowing blood, such as ants, cockroaches, fleas and so forth.

(3) Impurities Pardoned by the Shareeah

(1) Mud found in the streets.

(2) Small amounts of blood.

(3) Pus from a human or from an animal one is permitted to eat.

---

[1] This point was not mentioned in the original text but it is something that is agreed upon.—JZ

The Manner of Purifying [or Removing] Impurities

Impurities are purified [or removed] by washing, moistening, scrubbing or wiping, as follows:

The purification of clothing having impurities: If the impurity has some body or weight to it, it is to be rubbed and scraped off and then washed. If the impurity is wet or moist, then it is to be washed.

The urine of a weaning boy who does not yet eat solid foods needs simply to be moistened.

Impurities on the ground are to be physically removed and then water is poured over any liquid impurity.

Shoes are made pure by rubbing them or walking over pure areas.

Finished or polished items, such as glass, knives, tiles and similar items are cleaned by wiping them.

If a dog licks into a bowl, the bowl is to be washed seven times, one of them being with dirt.

Topic Four:
Etiquette and Cleaning Oneself After Relieving Oneself

The word *al-istinjaa* (الاستنجاء) means to remove the remains of one's feces or urine with water. The word *al-istijmaar* (الاستجمار) means to remove the remains of one's feces or urine with rocks, paper or something of that nature.

It is recommended for the person to enter the bathroom with his left foot first and to say,

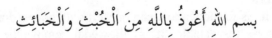

بِسْمِ اللهِ أَعُوذُ بِاللَّهِ مِنَ الْخُبْثِ وَالْخَبَائِثِ

"In the name of Allah. I seek refuge in Allah from the male and female devils."

Upon leaving the bathroom, it is recommended to step out with the right foot first and to say,

غُفْرَانَكَ الْحَمْدُ لِلَّهِ الَّذِي أَذْهَبَ عَنِّي الأَذَى وَعَافَانِي

"[I seek] Your forgiveness. All praise be to Allah who removed from me what is harmful and made me healthy."

It is recommended for the one who is relieving himself to lean on his left leg [meaning the left thigh]. It is also recommended for him to be out of the sight of the people and to conceal himself. For urination, he should choose a place that would prevent his urine from getting on to his clothing.

It is disliked to enter the bathroom with anything containing the name of Allah, unless there is some strong need to do so. One should also avoid raising one's clothing before getting close to the ground. One should also avoid speaking in the bathroom. He should also avoid touching his private part with his right hand or cleaning it with his right hand.

It is forbidden to face or have one's back toward the *qiblah* [the direction in which one prays] while relieving oneself in open lands. If one is in a building, it is permissible, although even then it is best to avoid it.

It is forbidden to urinate or defecate in the roadways, useful areas of shade, under a fruit-producing tree and similar other locations [in other words, any place that will bring harm or discomfort to others].

One should clean oneself with a clean rock, wiping oneself three times, if that totally cleans the person. If that does not clean the person, he should wipe himself more. It is recommended to make it an odd number of times, three, five and so forth.

It is forbidden to clean oneself with bones, dung, food or anything respectable. It is allowed to remove the remains with water, napkins or paper. To combine both water and rocks is better than to use water alone.

It is obligatory to wash with water the parts of one's clothing that have impurities on them. If one is not sure exactly where such places are, he is to wash the entire garment.

It is from the sunnah for a man to urinate sitting. It is not disliked for him to do so standing given that he can keep himself free from any impurities landing on him.

Topic Five:
The Acts Corresponding to the Nature of Humans (*Sunan al-Fitra*)

Definition

In essence, these are the acts that are consistent with the natural and original way that humans were fashioned to be. Hence, they are the acts that a human should fulfill in his life.

The *Sunan al-Fitra* (سنن الفطرة)

[These acts are the following]:

(1) Using the toothstick [or toothbrush]: It is recommend to use this at any time, as it is purifying for the mouth and pleasing to the Lord. However, it is even more emphasized while making ablution for prayer, before reading the Quran, upon entering the mosque or house, when rising from one's sleep and whenever one's breath has changed its smell.

(2) Shaving the pubic hairs, plucking the underarm hairs, trimming the [finger and toe] nails and washing the finger joints and knuckles.

(3) Trimming the moustache and allowing the beard to grow full and big.

(4) Treating the hair on one's head properly by oiling and combing it. It is disliked to shave part of the head while leaving the rest unshaved. This is considered a type of mutilation.

(5) Dyeing the gray hairs with henna or *katam* [a type of herb used in dyeing hair].

(6) Perfuming oneself with musk or something similar.

(7) Getting circumcised: This is the cutting off of the foreskin of the male organ so that filth and urine cannot build up there. With respect to the female, it is the cutting off of the tip of the clitoris, which looks like a seed. [It is not the same as what is known as "female genital mutilation," which implies the removal of the entire clitoris and which is forbidden.] It is known to those who specialize in this field. Circumcision is an act of purification and cleanliness. It has many advantages to it. It is a recommended act for males and a noble act for females.

Topic Six:
Ablution (*Wudhu*)

Definition of *al-Wudhu* (الوضوء)

Ablution is the use of purifying water [in washing] the four extremities [and the head] in the manner particularly prescribed by the Law.

The Virtues of *Wudhu*

The virtues of *wudhu* are indicated in the hadith of the Prophet (peace be upon him) which states,

مَا مِنْكُمْ مِنْ أَحَدٍ يَتَوَضَّأُ فَيُسْبِغُ الْوَضُوءَ ثُمَّ يَقُولُ أَشْهَدُ أَنْ لا
إِلَهَ إِلاَّ اللَّهُ وَأَنَّ مُحَمَّدًا عَبْدُ اللَّهِ وَرَسُولُهُ إِلاَّ فُتِحَتْ لَهُ أَبْوَابُ
الْجَنَّةِ الثَّمَانِيَةُ يَدْخُلُ مِنْ أَيِّهَا شَاءَ

"None of you makes ablution and completes the ablution fully and then says, 'I bear witness that none is worthy of worship except Allah and that Muhammad is the servant of Allah and His messenger,' except that opened for him will be the eight gates of Paradise and he enters from any of them he wishes." (Recorded by Muslim.)

Completing the washing fully of the extremities, without extravagance, entitles one to be among *al-ghurr al-muhajjaloon* on the Day of Resurrection. The Prophet (peace be upon him) said,

إِنَّ أُمَّتِي يُدْعَوْنَ يَوْمَ الْقِيَامَةِ غُرًّا مُحَجَّلِينَ مِنْ آثَارِ الْوُضُوءِ
فَمَنِ اسْتَطَاعَ مِنْكُمْ أَنْ يُطِيلَ غُرَّتَهُ فَلْيَفْعَلْ

"My nation will be called on the Day of Resurrection by the name *ghurr muhajjileen* [implying that the parts of the body will be glittering or radiant] due to the traces of ablution. Whoever among you who can lengthen his portions of radiance should do so." [Recorded by al-Bukhari and Muslim.]

The Prerequisites for the *Wudhu*

The prerequisites [or the required aspects that one must meet in order for his ablution to be valid] are ten:

(1) The person must be a Muslim.

(2) The person must be sane.

(3) The person must be old enough that he is able to discern matters.

(4) The person must have the intention to perform the ablution. This intention must remain with him throughout the act, in the sense that he may never have the intention to stop performing the ablution.

(5) The actions that require one to make ablution are no longer going on.

(6) *Al-istinjaa* or *al-istijmaar* [these are the washing of the remains of urine or feces after relieving oneself, as described earlier; these acts must have been performed prior if one had relieved himself since the last time he made ablution].

(7) The water being used must be of the "purifying" category.

(8) The water must be permissible [that is, received through permissible means].

(9) Anything that would keep the water from reaching the skin must first be removed.

(10) The time of the prayer must have begun for those people who are in a continual state of nullifying the ablution.[1]

Actions That Obligate the Making of Ablution

Ablution becomes obligatory after those acts that negate ablution [that shall be described shortly and before performing an act which requires one to be in a state of purity].

---

[1] For example, those suffering from enuresis (bladder control diseases) or a prolonged flow of blood from the vagina.

The Obligatory Acts of the Ablution

The obligatory acts in making ablution are six:
(1) Washing the face, including the mouth and nose.
(2) Washing the arms [from the hands] to the elbows.
(3) Wiping the head, including the ears.
(4) Washing the feet.
Allah has said,

يَاأَيُّهَا الَّذِينَ آمَنُوا إِذَا قُمْتُمْ إِلَى الصَّلَاةِ فَاغْسِلُوا وُجُوهَكُمْ وَأَيْدِيَكُمْ إِلَى الْمَرَافِقِ وَامْسَحُوا بِرُءُوسِكُمْ وَأَرْجُلَكُمْ إِلَى الْكَعْبَيْنِ

"O you who believe! When you prepare for prayer, wash your faces, and your hands (and arms) to the elbows; rub your heads (with water); and (wash) your feet to the ankles" (*al-Maaidah* 6), [thus establishing the above mentioned obligatory acts of the ablution].

(5) The above stated acts must be done in the proper order as Allah has mentioned them in order and has stated an act of wiping in between two parts that need to be washed.[1]

The Recommended Acts of the Ablution

(1) Using the toothstick (*siwaak*).
(2) Washing the hands [first] three times.
(3) Rinsing one's mouth and nose.
(4) Putting water through a thick beard and between the fingers and toes.
(5) Starting with the right side in all of the acts.

---

[1] The argument that the author is making is that if the order was not intended, all of the parts that are to be washed would be mentioned first and then what is to be wiped would be mentioned afterwards.—JZ

(6) Washing [the appropriate parts] two or three times.

(7) Using new water for the ears [that is, not just using the water leftover from wiping the head].

(8) The [specific] supplication that comes after the ablution.

(9) Praying two *rakat*s afterwards.

Disliked Acts Related to the Ablution

(1) Making ablution in a place that has impurities with the fear that such impurities may fall upon the person.

(2) Washing the different bodily parts more than three times. The Prophet (peace be upon him) said [after performing the ablution and washing each part three times],

$$فَمَنْ زَادَ عَلَى هَذَا فَقَدْ أَسَاءَ وَتَعَدَّى وَظَلَمَ$$

"[That is how the ablution is to be performed.] Whoever adds to that has done evil, transgressed and done wrong." (Recorded by al-Nasaai.[1])

(3) Being wasteful with respect to the amount of water used. The Messenger of Allah (peace be upon him) used to make ablution with an amount of water equivalent to what a person can hold with his two hands cupped together. Furthermore, extravagance and waste in any matter is prohibited.

(4) Leaving one or more of the recommended acts of the ablution. Not performing them means that one will miss the reward of that act and one should be very keen upon getting such rewards. Therefore, he should not leave that act.

---

[1] Recorded by al-Nasaai and others. According to al-Albaani, it is *hasan sahih*. See Muhammad Naasir al-Deen al-Albaani, *Saheeh Sunan al-Nasaai* (Riyadh: Maktab al-Tarbiyyah al-Arabi li-Duwal al-Khaleej, 1988), vol. 1, p. 31.—JZ

What Nullifies One's Ablution

(1) Anything that comes out of the body via the private parts.

(2) Losing consciousness [or sanity] through temporary insanity, fainting or intoxication.

(3) The person, him or herself, touching his or her sexual organ.

(4) A man touching a woman with desire or a woman touching a man with desire.

(5) Eating camel meat.

(6) Everything that obligates *ghusl* (the complete washing) also obligates ablution, such as accepting Islam, releasing sperm and so forth— except for death which mandates *ghusl* only and not ablution.

[(7) A sound sleep.[1]]

Topic Seven:

Ghusl or Complete Washing

The Lexical and Technical Definition of *Ghusl*

Lexically, *ghusl* (غسل) is the water; *ghasl* is the act; and *ghisl* is the cleaning agent.

Technically, it refers to putting water over all of the body, from the top of the head to the bottom of the feet, with purifying water in the specified manner. Men and women are the same with respect to *ghusl* except that after menses or post-partum bleeding, the woman must completely remove all of

---

[1] For some reason, perhaps simply a printing mistake, this was not included in the Arabic text but it is definitely one of the agreed upon and established acts nullifying the ablution.— JZ

the traces of blood and clean that area with something that will remove the scent of the blood.

The Acts That Obligate *Ghusl*

(1) Ejaculation of sperm due to sensual pleasure.

(2) Placing of the man's sexual organ into the woman's sexual organ.

(3) If a Muslim dies, *ghusl* must be made on his body, except in the case of the one who dies as a martyr on the battlefield.

(4) A non-Muslim becoming Muslim or an apostate repenting.

(5) Menstruation.

(6) Post-partum bleeding.

Acts For Which *Ghusl* is Recommended

(1) The Friday Prayer.

(2) Upon entering into the inviolable state of the pilgrimage.

(3) By the one who washed the dead body.

(4) For the Eid Prayers.

(5) Upon losing one's consciousness through temporary insanity or fainting.

(6) For entering into Makkah.

(7) For the eclipse prayer and the prayer for rain.

(8) For each prayer by the woman who has a prolonged flow of blood.

(9) For any type of social gathering.

The Prerequisites of the *Ghusl*

[The following must be met for the *ghusl* to be considered proper:]

(1) The factor obligating the *ghusl* has stopped, for example, the menses have come to an end, the sexual fluid has been all emitted.

(2) Intention.

(3) Being a Muslim.

(4) Being sane.

(5) Being beyond the age of discernment.

(6) Permissible, purifying water.

(7) Having the water reach the skin.

The Mandatory Acts of the *Ghusl*

One must mention the name of Allah. If one forgets it, it is then overlooked but it is not pardonable if one intentionally does not mention it.

The Obligatory Acts of the *Ghusl*

The obligatory aspects are the intention and ensuring that the water reaches all of the parts of the body, including inside the mouth and nose. It is sufficient for one to suspect [without absolute certainty] that the water has reached all the parts.

If a person intends both a recommended or obligatory *ghusl*, then one [act of *ghusl*] suffices for the other.

If a person needs to make *ghusl* for both sexual defilement and menses, one *ghusl* with one intention suffices.

The Recommended Acts of the *Ghusl*

(1) Mentioning the name of Allah.

(2) Beginning by first removing any filth from one's body.

(3) Washing one's hands before entering them into the water container.

(4) Making ablution first.

(5) Beginning with the right side of one's body.

(6) Following each act immediately with the succeeding act.

(7) Passing one's [wet] hand over the remainder of one's body.

(8) Rewashing the feet in a separate place.

Disliked Acts Related to the *Ghusl*

(1) Wasting water or using it extravagantly.

(2) Washing in an impure place.

(3) Washing without having some kind of barrier [that prevents others from seeing the person].

(4) Making *ghusl* in stagnant water.

Acts Forbidden for the Person Required to Make *Ghusl*

(1) Prayer.

(2) Circumambulating the Kaabah.

(3) Touching or carrying the Quran except in its container.

(4) Sitting in the mosque.

Topic Eight:
Tayammum

Lexical and Technical Definition

Lexically, *tayammum* (تيمم) means intent, purpose and aim. Technically, it refers to wiping the face and hands with clean soil in a particular fashion. It is from the things that have been sanctioned by Allah only for this Nation [the followers of the Prophet Muhammad (peace be upon him)]. It is a substitute for purifying with water.

Who is Allowed to Resort to *Tayammum*

(1) The one who has no water available to him, either because it is not present or it is far away.

(2) The one who has an injury or disease and he fears that water may cause him more harm.

(3) The one who only has extremely cold water available to him and he has no means to heat it.

(4) The person who is in need of his water for himself or others to drink and he fears dying of thirst.

Prerequisites for the Obligation of *Tayammum*

(1) The person involved must be adult.

(2) The person must have the means to use the soil [in the way described below].

(3) The act obliging ablution [or *ghusl*] has occurred.

Conditions for the Soundness of the *Tayammum*

(1) Being Muslim.

(2) Ending of the bleeding of menstruation or post-partum bleeding.

(3) Being sane.

(4) The presence of pure soil.

The Obligatory Portions of the *Tayammum*

(1) Intention.

(2) Pure soil.

(3) The first strike on the earth.

(4) Wiping the face and hands.

The Recommended Portions of the *Tayammum*

(1) Mentioning the name of Allah.

(2) Facing the *qiblah*.

(3) Performing it when one is intending to pray.

(4) A second striking of the earth.

(5) Performing the acts in the proper order.

(6) Performing the acts one after the other.

(7) Putting the fingers through each other.

What Negates the *Tayammum*

(1) The existence of water.

(2) It is nullified by all the things previously mentioned that nullify the ablution; similarly, what nullifies the *ghusl* also nullifies the *tayammum*. This is because it is a replacement for them and what nullifies the replaced act also nullifies its replacement.

The Manner in Which *Tayammum* is Performed

The person has the intention, then mentions the name of Allah, then strikes the soil with his hands and wipes them over his face and hands in the proper order and right after the other.

Tayammum for Casts and Injuries

If a person has a broken bone or wound and he fears that he will harm himself by washing and it is difficult for him to wipe over those areas, then he may make *tayammum* for them and wash the remaining parts of his body.

If a person has no access to water or soil, he may pray in whatever situation he is and he does not have to later repeat his prayer.

Topic Nine:

Wiping Over Leather Sandals, [Socks] or Splints

(1) Ibn al-Mubaarak, "There is no difference of opinion about [the permissibility] of wiping over the sandals." Imam Ahmad said, "There are no [qualms] in my heart about wiping over the sandals. There are forty hadith from the Messenger of Allah (peace be upon him) about it." He [Imam Ahmad] also said, "It is better than washing because he [the Prophet (peace be upon him)] used to seek doing it and they would only seek what is best."

(2) Its time length: For the non-traveler, he may wipe over his sandals for a period of one day and night. The traveler may do it for three days with their nights. This timing begins with the first time a person invalidates his ablution after wearing his sandals.

(3) Its prerequisites: What is being worn is permissible and pure, covering the required area, staying up on its own and put on while in a state of purity.

(4) The manner in which to wipe over the sandals: The person puts his hand into the water and wipes the top of the sock from the toes to the back [of the top of the foot], one time, without wiping the bottom of them or the heels.

(5) What negates the wiping: (a) Removing the piece of clothing from the foot; (b) what requires one to make *ghusl*, such as sexual defilement; (c) having a large hole in them, beyond what is customarily acceptable; (d) the permissible time limit expiring.

It is permissible to wipe over a cast wherever it may be and no matter how long it may be there, even if one becomes sexually defiled.

Chapter Two: The Prayer (*Al-Salaat*)

This chapter is comprised of an introduction and the following eight topics:

Topic One: Some rulings related to the prayer;
Topic Two: Prayer in congregation;
Topic Three: Shortening and combining the prayers;
Topic Four: Voluntary prayers;
Topic Five: The Friday Prayer;
Topic Six: The Eid Prayers;
Topic Seven: The prayer for rain and the eclipse prayers;
Topic Eight: The funeral prayer.

Introduction

Lexical and Technical Definition

Linguistically, the word *al-salaat* (الصلاة) means supplication. Allah says,

$$\text{وَصَلِّ عَلَيْهِمْ إِنَّ صَلَاتَكَ سَكَنٌ لَهُمْ}$$

"Supplicate on their behalf, verily your supplications are a source of security for them" (*al-Taubah* 103). Technically, the word refers to specific statements and actions beginning with the *takbeer* (saying "*Allahu akbar*") and ending with the salutations with its particular prerequisites.

Its Obligatory Nature

The prayer was made obligatory during the Night of Ascension to heaven before the migration to Madinah. It is one of the pillars of Islam. It was the first act required by the Prophet (peace be upon him) after proper belief in Allah. The Messenger of Allah (peace be upon him) said,

رَأْسُ الأَمْرِ الإِسْلاَمُ وَعَمُودُهُ الصَّلاَةُ وَذِرْوَةُ سَنَامِهِ الْجِهَادُ

"The head of the matter is Islam. Its pillar is prayer. And its apex is jihad."[1]

The Wisdom Behind Its Legislation

Prayer is in gratitude to the great blessings that Allah has bestowed upon his servants. Similarly, it is one of the clearest demonstrations of the meaning of worship, as it displays one turning to Allah and submission and humility in front of Him and a private conversation with Quranic reciting, words of remembrance and supplications. Furthermore, it establishes a relationship and connection between the servant and his Lord; by it, the person rises above the materialistic world [and moves on] to the purification of the soul and its tranquillity. Furthermore, [in this world,] the person becomes immersed in the throngs of life and its attractions and the prayer rescues him before he becomes drowned and, instead, places him in front of the reality of which he was beforehand negligent. He realizes that there is something greater [than this life]. He realizes that this life could not have been created with such perfection and [this world] subjugated to mankind just so that man can live a life of uselessness, without purpose, just moving from one pleasure to another. [Instead, there must be a

---

[1] An authentic hadith recorded by Ahmad, al-Tirmidhi and others.—JZ

much greater purpose: the worship of Allah and His pleasure in the Hereafter.]

Topic One:

Some Regulations Related to Prayer

The Ruling Concerning the Prayer and The Number of Prayers

Prayer is of two types: obligatory and voluntary.

The obligatory prayers are also divided into two categories: prayers obligatory upon each and every individual and prayers only obligatory on the community as a whole.

The prayers that are obligatory upon each individual are those obligatory upon every legally capable man or woman; these are the five daily prayers. Allah says,

$$ إِنَّ الصَّلاةَ كَانَتْ عَلَى الْمُؤْمِنِينَ كِتَابًا مَوْقُوتًا $$

"Verily, the prayers are enjoined on the believers at stated times" (*al-Nisaa* 103). Allah also says,

$$ وَمَا أُمِرُوا إِلاَّ لِيَعْبُدُوا اللَّهَ مُخْلِصِينَ لَهُ الدِّينَ حُنَفَاءَ وَيُقِيمُوا الصَّلاةَ وَيُؤْتُوا الزَّكَاةَ وَذَلِكَ دِينُ الْقَيِّمَةِ $$

"And they have been commanded no more than this: to worship Allah, offering Him sincere devotion, being true (in faith), and to establish regular prayer, and to pay the *zakaat*, and that is the religion right and straight" (*al-Bayyinah* 5).

The Messenger of Allah (peace be upon him) said,

بُنِيَ الإِسْلامُ عَلَى خَمْسٍ شَهَادَةِ أَنْ لا إِلَهَ إِلا اللَّهُ وَأَنَّ مُحَمَّدًا
رَسُولُ اللَّهِ وَإِقَامِ الصَّلاةِ وَإِيتَاءِ الزَّكَاةِ وَالْحَجِّ الْبَيْتِ وَصَوْمِ
رَمَضَانَ

"Islam is built upon five [pillars]: testifying that there is none
worthy of worship except Allah and that Muhammad is the
Messenger of Allah, establishing the prayers, giving the
zakaat, making the pilgrimage to the House and fasting the
month of Ramadhaan." (Recorded by al-Bukhari.) Naafi ibn
al-Azraq said to ibn Abbas [the Companion of the Prophet
(peace be upon him)], "Do you find the five [daily] prayers in
the Quran." He responded, "Yes," and then recited the verse,

فَسُبْحَانَ اللَّهِ حِينَ تُمْسُونَ وَحِينَ تُصْبِحُونَ وَلَهُ الْحَمْدُ فِي
السَّمَاوَاتِ وَالأَرْضِ وَعَشِيًّا وَحِينَ تُظْهِرُونَ

"So (give) glory to Allah, when you reach the evening [for the
sunset and the night prayers] and when you rise in the
morning; to Him be praise, in the heavens and on earth; and in
the late afternoon and when the day begins to decline [for the
noon prayer]" (al-Room 17-18).

In the hadith of the bedouin, he came to the Messenger
of Allah (peace be upon him) and said, "Concerning the
prayers, what has Allah made obligatory upon us?" The
Messenger of Allah answered, "Five prayers." The bedouin
said, "Are there any other prayers obligatory on us?" He
replied, "No, unless you do so voluntarily." (Recorded by al-
Bukhari and Muslim.)

The prayers that are obligatory upon the community as
a whole include the other [obligatory] prayers and aspects
[related to the prayers], such as the call to prayer, the eclipse
prayer and funeral prayer.

Ordering the Young to Pray

When the youth reach the age of seven, they should be ordered to pray. When they are ten, they should be disciplined by a mild beating if they do not pray. This is based on the hadith,

مُرُوا أَبْنَاءَكُمْ بِالصَّلاةِ لِسَبْعِ سِنِينَ وَاضْرِبُوهُمْ عَلَيْهَا لِعَشْرِ سِنِينَ وَفَرِّقُوا بَيْنَهُمْ فِي الْمَضَاجِعِ

"Order your children to pray at the age of seven and beat them to do so at the age of ten and separate them in their bedding." (Recorded by Ahmad and Abu Dawood.[1])

The Ruling Concerning One Who Denies the Obligation of Prayer

Whoever denies the obligatory nature of prayers has committed an act of unbelief— if he was a person who was not ignorant— even if he performs the prayer. This is because he is belying Allah, His Messenger (peace be upon him) and the consensus of the Muslim Nation. The same ruling applies for the one who abandons the prayer due to being lackadaisical or lazy, even if he believes in its obligatory nature. Allah has said,

---

[1] According to al-Albaani, this hadith is *hasan*. See al-Albaani, *Saheeh al-Jaami*, vol. 2, pp. 1021-1022.—JZ

فَاقْتُلُوا الْمُشْرِكِينَ حَيْثُ وَجَدْتُمُوهُمْ وَخُذُوهُمْ وَاحْصُرُوهُمْ
وَاقْعُدُوا لَهُمْ كُلَّ مَرْصَدٍ فَإِنْ تَابُوا وَأَقَامُوا الصَّلَاةَ وَآتَوْا
الزَّكَاةَ فَخَلُّوا سَبِيلَهُمْ إِنَّ اللَّهَ غَفُورٌ رَحِيمٌ

"Then fight and slay the pagans wherever you find them, and
seize them, beleaguer them, and lie in wait for them in every
stratagem (of war); but if they repent, and establish regular
prayers and pay the *zakaat*, then open the way for them: for
Allah is Oft-Forgiving, Most Merciful" (*al-Taubah* 5). Jaabir
(may Allah be pleased with him) narrated that the Messenger
of Allah (peace be upon him) said,

إِنَّ بَيْنَ الرَّجُلِ وَبَيْنَ الشِّرْكِ وَالْكُفْرِ تَرْكَ الصَّلَاةِ

"Between a man and polytheism (*al-shirk*) and disbelief (*al-kufr*) is the abandoning of the prayer." (Recorded by Muslim.)

The Essential Components (*Arkaan*) of the Prayer

There are fourteen essential components or *arkaan*
(أركان) of the prayer which may not be left, not intentionally,
forgetfully or ignorantly.[1]

(1) Standing straight in the obligatory prayer for the
one who has the ability to do so.

(2) The opening *takbeer* which is the statement,
"*Allahu akbar,*" and nothing else suffices for the beginning of
the prayer.

(3) Reciting *soorah al-Faatihah.*

---

[1] Essential components (*arkaan*) differ from obligatory acts (*waajibaat*). If a person fails
to perform the essential components, under most circumstances it will be as if he did not
perform the act at all. If a person fails to perform the obligatory acts, under some
circumstances he may simply have to make up for those acts in another way.—JZ

(4) The bow.

(5) Rising from the bow and standing up straight.

(6) Prostration.

(7) Coming up from the prostration.

(8) Sitting between the two acts of prostration.

(9) Having calmness and stillness [in each of the acts of the prayer].

(10) The final *tashahud*.[1]

(11) Sitting for the final *tashahud*.

(12) Saying the prayers for the Prophet Muhammad (peace be upon him).

(13) Saying the salutation. This is to say twice, "*Assalaam alaikum wa rahmatullaahi* (peace be upon you and the mercy of Allah)." It is best not to add, "*wa baarakatuhu* (and his blessings)" for in the hadith of ibn Masood, he narrated that the Prophet (peace be upon him) would greet on his right, "*Assalaam alaikum wa rahmatullaahi* (peace be upon you and the mercy of Allah)" and on his left, "*Assalaam alaikum wa rahmatullaahi* (peace be upon you and the mercy of Allah)." (Recorded by Muslim.)

(14) Performing the above in the correct order.

The Obligatory Acts (*Waajibaat*) of the Prayer

There are eight obligatory or *waajibaat* (واجبات) acts of the prayer:

(1) The *takbeer*s other than the opening *takbeer*.

(2) Saying, "*Sami-Allaahu liman hamidah* (Allah has heard him who praises Him)," for both the Imam and the one who prays alone.

(3) Saying, "*Rabbanaa wa lakal-hamd* (Our Lord and to you is the praise)."

---

[1] These are the first set of words recited while sitting, beginning with the words *al-tahiyaatu-lilaahi*...

(4) Saying, "*Subhanna Rabbiyal-Adheem* (Exalted and perfect is my Lord, the Great)," at least once while bowing.

(5) Saying, "*Subhanna Rabbiyal-Ala* (Exalted and perfect is my Lord, the Most High)," at least once while prostrating.

(6) Saying the first *tashahud*.

(7) Sitting for the first *tashahud*.

The prayer is nullified if any of these are left intentionally. The prayer is not nullified if they are left forgetfully or ignorantly.

The Prerequisites for the Prayer

Shuroot (prerequisites, conditions) lexically means a sign. Technically, it refers to something, say X, that Y cannot exist without; however, the mere existence of X does not necessarily mean that Y will occur.

The prerequisites of the prayer are:

(1) Intention.

(2) Being Muslim.

(3) Being sane.

(4) Being at least of the age of discernment.

(5) The time for the prayer having begun.

(6) Being in a state of purity.

(7) Facing the *qiblah*.

(8) Covering the private parts.

(9) Being free of any physical impurities [on one's clothing or place where one is praying].

The Timings for the Five Daily Prayers

The timings show the limits for the prayer. The time is a cause mandating the obligation of the prayer and it is one of the prerequisites for the prayer.

The Prophet (peace be upon him) delineated the timings of the five daily prayers in more than one hadith. Ibn Abbaas narrated that the Prophet (peace be upon him) said, "[The angel] Gabriel led me in the prayers at the House [of Allah] on two [days]." Then he mentioned the timings of the prayers and he then said, "Then Gabriel turned to me and said, 'O Muhammad, this is the timing of the prophets before you and your timings are between these two [extremes that he had shown the Prophet (peace be upon him)].'" Recorded by Abu Dawood.[1]

The five daily prayers are divided between the day and night. If a person gets his portion of sleep such that he is rested and the morning time is approaching, the time for work and seriousness, the time of the Fajr prayer also comes. This is so that humans consciously realize that they are different from the remainder of the creation. He faces his day and his faith has been increased.

When midday comes, he stops again to ponder over his day with his Lord in the Dhuhr Prayer and in order to correct his deeds of the beginning of the day. As mid-afternoon comes, he prays his prayer, facing with it the rest of his day. Then the Maghrib (Sunset) comes. In front of him is the night and the [Sunset and] Isha Prayers during it will carry him through the night, although it is the time of hidden acts, with light and guidance to the sound path. Furthermore, the prayer, in its varied times, is an opportunity to ponder over Allah's dominion and His perfection concerning everything that encompasses man in his night and day.

The Time of the Dhuhr Prayer. The time of the Dhuhr Prayer begins when the sun passes the meridian or its zenith. The ending of the time for Dhuhr is when the shadow of something is equal to the thing's length in the afternoon.

---

[1] According to al-Albaani, this hadith is *hasan sahih*. See Muhammad Naasir al-Deen al-Albaani, *Sahih Sunan Abi Dawood* (Riyadh: Maktab al-Tarbiyyah al-Arabi li-Duwal al-Khaleej, 1989), vol. 1, p. 79.—JZ

The Time of the Asr Prayer. The beginning of the time for the Asr Prayer is when the shadow of something is equal to its length in the afternoon, as such is when the time for the Dhuhr Prayer comes to an end. As for the ending of the time of the Asr Prayer, the choice time by which to pray it is when the shadow of something is twice its own length. However, if necessary, it may be prayed all the way up until [just before] the sun sets.

The Time of the Maghrib Prayer. The beginning of the time for the Maghrib Prayer is when the sun sets. Its final time is when the stars become numerous and form clusters with one another. However, its actual final time, although it is disliked to delay it until this time, is when the twilight is finished.

The Time of the Isha Prayer. Its earliest time is when the twilight has disappeared. Its ending time is when half of the night has passed.

The Time of the Fajr Prayer. Its earliest time is at the second [or true] dawn and its ending time is sunrise.

The Timings for the Prayers in Very Northern or Southern Lands

The lands of extreme latitudes are divided into three categories:

(1) Those lands that are between 45° and 48° north or south of the equator; in these lands, the signs of the day and night are very apparent, of long or short lengths.

(2) Those lands that are between 48° and 66° north or south of the equator; in these lands, some of the signs of the day and night are not apparent during portions of the year. For example, the twilight may continue to exist until nearly the time of Fajr.

(3) Those lands that are from beyond 66° north or south of the equator until the respective poles; in these lands,

the daily signs of night and day are not visible for long periods of the year.

The Rulings Concerning Each of These Lands. As for the lands in category (1), it is obligatory upon their inhabitants to perform the prayers in their specified times, as were described above. As for those lands in category (3), there is no difference of opinion that their inhabitants must estimate or approximate the timings of the prayers. This is analogous to the case of estimating the times of the prayers during the time of the Anti-Messiah (Dajjaal). In the hadith, the Prophet (peace be upon him) was asked how long the anti-Messiah would be on the earth. In the response, he said, "A day like a year." The Companions asked, "That day which is like a year, is it sufficient for us to pray [the prayer of] a day and night?" He answered, "No, you must estimate [the times for the prayers]." (Recorded by Muslim.) There is a difference of opinion as to how they should approximate the timings. Some say that they should follow the timings of the closest land that has the regular signs of day and night and follow those proper signs for the timings of the prayers. Perhaps that is the strongest opinion. Some say that they should approximate them with the timing of a temperate zone, where the night is treated as twelve hours as is the daytime. Some say that they should estimate the prayers according to the timing of Makkah or Madinah.

As for the lands in the second category, their timings for the prayers other than the *Isha* and *Fajr* Prayers will be the same as those in the first category [that is, they pray according to what they see]. As for the *Isha* and *Fajr* Prayers, their ruling is the same as for those in the third category [that is, they must estimate the times for those prayers].

Topic Two:
Congregational Prayer

Wisdom Behind Its Legislation

The congregational prayer is from the most important acts of obedience to Allah and one of the greatest acts of worship. Furthermore, it is a great show of togetherness, mercy and equality between the Muslims, as they gather together in a small convention five times in a day and night, in a noble fashion, under one person's leadership and all facing one direction. The hearts come together and are purified; mercy and relationships are strengthened; and the differences flow away.

The Ruling Concerning Congregational Prayer

The prayer in congregation is obligatory upon the free, capable men, whether resident or traveling. This is based on Allah's statement,

وَإِذَا كُنتَ فِيهِمْ فَأَقَمْتَ لَهُمُ الصَّلاةَ فَلْتَقُمْ طَائِفَةٌ مِنْهُمْ مَعَكَ

"When you (O Messenger) are with them, and stand to lead them in prayer, let one party of them stand up (in prayer) with you" (al-Nisaa 102).[1] The command [in the verse] implies obligation. If that is the case while in a state of fear, [the

---

[1] As is clear from the remainder of this verse that the author did not quote in full, this verse is about praying while on the battlefield. Hence, the conclusion that the author makes above.—JZ

obligation to pray in congregation] must more so be the case in a time of safety.

What Constitutes a Congregational Prayer

A congregational prayer is made up of [as a minimum] an Imam and a follower, even if it be a woman. This is based on the hadith narrated by Abu Musa,

$$ اثْنَانِ فَمَا فَوْقَهُمَا جَمَاعَةٌ $$

"Two and any [number] above that are a congregation." (Recorded by ibn Maajah.[1])

The Place Where the Congregational Prayer is to Be Held

It is the recommended practice to perform the congregational prayer in the mosque. However, it is permissible to pray it elsewhere if need requires that. The women may also pray in congregation separately from the men, as Aisha and Umm Salamah (as al-Daraqutni recorded) used to do. The Prophet (peace be upon him) ordered Umm Waraqah to lead her household in prayer. (Recorded by Abu Dawood.)

---

[1] According to al-Albaani, this hadith is weak. See Muhammad Naasir al-Deen al-Albaani, *Dhaeef al-Jaami al-Sagheer* (Beirut: al-Maktab al-Islaami, 1988), p. 22.—JZ

Topic Three:
Shortening and Combining Prayers

The Meaning of Shortening the Prayers

Shortening the prayers while traveling means to perform the four *rakat* prayers as only two *rakah*s. This law is related to the great aspect of the Shareeah of taking into consideration the needs and circumstances of the Muslim and to make things easier upon him. Shortening the prayers is sanctioned in the Book of Allah, sunnah and is permissible according to the agreement of the leading scholars.

Shortening the Prayers Generally, While in a State of Security or Otherwise

The prayer is shortened while traveling, regardless of whether one is in a state of security or fear. The fear that is mentioned in the verse[1] is only referring to the usual case at that time because most of the Prophet's journeys were conducted while there was reason to fear the enemy. Ali once said to Umar, "Do we still shorten the prayer even though we are in a state of security?" Umar said, "I was surprised by the same thing that you are surprised at so I asked the Prophet (peace be upon him) and he said,

صَدَقَةٌ تَصَدَّقَ اللَّهُ بِهَا عَلَيْكُمْ فَاقْبَلُوا صَدَقَتَهُ

---

[1] The verse related to shortening one's prayer while traveling is, "When you travel through the earth, there is no blame on you if you shorten your prayers, for fear the unbelievers may attack you: for the unbelievers are unto you open enemies" (*al-Nisaa* 101).—JZ

"This is a charity that Allah has bestowed upon you, so accept His charity." (Recorded by Muslim.)

The Distance That Allows One to Shorten the Prayer While Traveling

The distance which allows one to shorten one's prayer while traveling is whatever is termed "traveling" according to the convention of the people and which also involves some form of transportation and taking along one's provisions.

When One Begins to Shorten the Prayer

The person begins to shorten his prayer as soon as he leaves the buildings of his city [while on a trip that can be considered "traveling"], according to the conventional usage of the term "leaving from". This is concluded because Allah has tied shortening the prayer with "going out through the land" and one does not "go out through the land" until he leaves the buildings of his area.

Combining the Prayers

Combining the prayers is an exceptional permission that is resorted to upon need. Many scholars recommend not combining the prayers unless there is some clear need to do so because the Prophet (peace be upon him) did not combine his prayers except on a small number of occasions. Everything that allows a person to shorten his prayers allows him to combine his prayers. However, not everything that leads to the permission of combining the prayers means that it is also permissible to shorten the prayers.

Combining at the Earlier or the Later Time

It is best for the person to do what is easier for him with respect to combining at the earlier of the two prayer times or at the later time. This is because the goal of combining the prayers is to make matters easy and simpler upon the person. If the two cases are equivalent [with respect to ease], then it is better to combine the prayers at the time of the later prayer. If a person is stopped at a location, the sunnah is to pray every prayer in its proper time.

[Topic:]
The Prostrations of Forgetfulness[1]

Al-sahu in the prayer means forgetfulness. The prostrations of forgetfulness are part of the law, according to the agreement of the leading scholars, for whoever does something [in the prayer] out of forgetfulness. This is based on both the action and the command of the Prophet (peace be upon him). It is proper to perform it whenever anyone has added anything, left anything out or became doubtful as to an act that he has performed in the prayer. It can be performed before the salutations or after them. They are two prostrations, without any *tashahud* between them, and one says *Allahu akbar* for every prostration and then makes the salutations after them.

---

[1] The Arabic text has included this as a subtopic under shortening the prayers but that arrangement has not been followed here as it is a topic on its own, independent of the question of shortening or combining the prayers.—JZ

Topic Four:
Voluntary Prayers

The Wisdom Behind Their Legislation

It is from the blessings of Allah upon His servants that He has established for them acts of worship that correspond to their natural human inclination and fulfill what He wants of performing the deeds in the proper manner. Since mankind is always open to mistakes and shortcomings, Allah has sanctioned what will complete their acts and will be a substitute for them. Among such sanctioned acts are the voluntary prayers. It is confirmed from the Messenger of Allah (peace be upon him) that the voluntary prayers complete the obligatory prayers when the person has not performed them in their complete sense.

The Best Voluntary Acts

The best act one can perform voluntarily is jihad for the sake of Allah. Next [in virtuousness comes] learning the knowledge of the religion. Allah says,

يَرْفَعِ اللَّهُ الَّذِينَ آمَنُوا مِنْكُمْ وَالَّذِينَ أُوتُوا الْعِلْمَ دَرَجَاتٍ

"Allah will raise up, to (suitable) ranks (and degrees), those of you who believe and who have been granted knowledge" (*al-Mujaadilah* 11). Then comes the prayer, which is the most virtuous act of the body. The Messenger of Allah (peace be upon him) said,

اسْتَقِيمُوا وَلَنْ تُحْصُوا وَاعْلَمُوا أَنَّ خَيْرَ أَعْمَالِكُمُ الصَّلَاةَ

"Adhere to the straight path. And you will not be able to do so [in all of your affairs]. And know that the best of your deeds is the prayer." (Recorded by ibn Maajah.[1])

Some of the Voluntary Prayers:

The Late-Night Prayers

The [voluntary] prayers of the night are better than those of the day. The last half of the night is better than the earlier half. This is based on the Prophet's statement,

$$\text{إِذَا مَضَى شَطْرُ اللَّيْلِ أَوْ ثُلْثَاهُ يَنْزِلُ اللَّهُ تَبَارَكَ وَتَعَالَى إِلَى السَّمَاءِ الدُّنْيَا}$$

"After half of the night or two-thirds of it have passed, our Lord, the Blessed and Exalted, descends to the lowest heaven..." (Recorded by Muslim.)

[This late night prayer is known as *tahajjud*.] The *tahajjud* is what is prayed after one has first slept. Aisha said, "The *tahajjud* is the standing for prayer after first sleeping."

The Dhuha Prayer

[The Dhuha Prayer is a prayer that is performed sometime after the sun has risen a little bit on the horizon until just before high noon.]

It is preferable to pray the Dhuha prayer on some days and to leave it on others. This is based on the hadith of Abu

---

[1] According to al-Albaani, this hadith is *sahih*. See al-Albaani, *Saheeh al-Jaami*, vol. 1, p. 225.—JZ

Saeed who said, "The Prophet (peace be upon him) used to pray the Dhuha prayer so often that we would say, 'He does not abandon it.' [Yet on other occasions] he would leave it so much that we would say, 'He does not pray it.'" (Recorded by Ahmad and by al-Tirmidhi who said, "It is *hasan ghareeb*."[1])

As a minimum, it is two *rakats*. The Prophet (peace be upon him) prayed it as four or six or, as a maximum, eight *rakats*. It is not a condition to be persistent in performing this prayer.

The Prayer for "Greeting" the Mosque

It is sunnah to pray what is known as the prayer of "greeting the mosque". This is based on the hadith from Abu Qataadah in which the Prophet (peace be upon him) said,

إِذَا دَخَلَ أَحَدُكُمُ الْمَسْجِدَ فَلَا يَجْلِسْ حَتَّى يُصَلِّيَ رَكْعَتَيْنِ

"When any of you enters the mosque, he should not sit until he prays two *rakats*." (Recorded by al-Bukhari, Muslim, Abu Dawood, al-Tirmidhi, al-Nasaai, ibn Maajah and Ahmad.)

Prostration While Reading [Specific Verses] of the Quran

It is recommended for the one reading the Quran and the one listening to prostrate [after reading specific verses of the Quran] and to say, "*Allaahu akbar*," upon prostrating and to make the salutations upon rising from the prostration. One should say while prostrating, "*Subhaana Rabbiya-l-Ala*

---

[1] According to al-Albaani, this hadith is weak. See Muhammad Naasir al-Deen al-Albaani, *Dhaeef Sunan al-Tirmidhi* (Beirut: al-Maktab al-Islaami, 1991), p. 53.—JZ

(Perfect and exalted is my Lord, the Most High)" or the other words that have been recorded.

Prostration of Thankfulness

It is recommended to make the prostration of thankfulness whenever a blessing comes to a person or some evil is repelled. This is based on the hadith from Abu Bakr who said, "Whenever news that pleased the Prophet (peace be upon him) came to him, he would quickly go down in prostration." (Recorded by Abu Dawood, al-Tirmidhi and ibn Maajah.[1]) Ali prostrated when he found Dhu al-Thidayah of the Khawarij [dead]. (Recorded by Ahmad.) Kaab ibn Maalik prostrated when he received the news of Allah accepting his repentance. (Recorded by al-Bukhari and Muslim.) Its characteristics and rulings are the same as that for the prostration of recitation.

The *Taraweeh* Prayer

The *taraweeh* prayer is an emphasized sunnah of the Messenger of Allah (peace be upon him). It is prayed in congregation in the mosque after the Night (*Isha*) Prayer during the month of Ramadhaan. The Messenger of Allah (peace be upon him) established this prayer and Umar ibn al-Khataab revived it [as one congregational prayer] during his time as the caliph. It is best to perform it as eleven *rakat*s but there is no harm in praying more than that. During the last ten nights [of Ramadhaan], one should try to increase his efforts in prayer, remembrance and supplications.

---

[1] According to al-Albaani, this hadith is *hasan*. See al-Albaani, *Saheeh al-Jaami*, vol. 2, p. 858.—JZ

The *Witr* Prayer

The *Witr* prayer is an emphasized sunnah that the Prophet (peace be upon him) performed and ordered to be performed. As a minimum, it is one *rakah*. However, its minimum for a more complete form is actually three *rakat*s. Its maximum is eleven *rakat*s.

The time for the Witr Prayer: Its time is from after the Night (*Isha*) Prayer until before the dawn of *Fajr*. It is recommended to make *qunoot* (supplications) after the bowing [of the last *rakah*].

Its description: [It may be prayed in any of the following fashions:]

(1) Praying [all the *rakat*s] together, without sitting for the *tashahud* except in the last *rakah*;

(2) Sitting for the *tashahud* [in the next to] last *rakah* and then standing without making the salutations and performing one *rakah* with a *tashahud* and salutations.

(3) Performing every two *rakat*s individually, with salutations at the end of them, and then ending them with one *rakah* which contains a *tashahud* and salutations. This manner is manner as it was the one that the Prophet (peace be upon him) performed [often] and repeatedly adhered to.

The Regular [Daily] Sunnah Prayers

The best of the daily sunnah prayers is the sunnah before the Dawn (*Fajr*) Prayer. Aisha narrated that the Messenger of Allah (peace be upon him) said,

رَكْعَتَا الْفَجْرِ خَيْرٌ مِنَ الدُّنْيَا وَمَا فِيهَا

"The two *rakat*s of *Fajr* [before the obligatory *Fajr* Prayer] are better than the world and what it contains." (Recorded by Muslim and by al-Tirmidhi who declared it authentic.)

The emphasized daily sunnah prayers are twelve in number: four *rakat*s before the Noon (*Dhuhr*) Prayer and two after it, two *rakat*s after the Sunset (*Maghrib*) Prayer, two *rakat*s after the Night (*Isha*) Prayer and the two *rakat*s before Fajr.

It is recommended to make up the daily sunnah prayers if one misses them. *Witr* is also to be made up but with an even number of *rakat*s during the daytime. However, if a person has missed a lot of obligatory prayers, he must busy himself with making those up first and not the sunnah prayers as it may cause him some hardship to make up both. However, he should also make up the two *rakat*s of sunnah for the *Fajr* Prayer due to their importance.

Finally, to perform these prayers in one's house is best, as opposed to the obligatory prayers which should be prayed in congregation [in the mosque].

Topic Five:

The Friday Prayer

The Virtue of Friday

Friday is among the best of days. For that reason, Allah has particularly guided this Nation to it and sanctioned their gathering to be on this day. The wisdom behind that includes an opportunity for the Muslims to get together, know each other, bond together and display mercy and assistance for one another. Friday is like a weekly celebration or festival. It is the best day upon which the sun rises.

The Status of the Friday Prayer

The Friday Prayer is obligatory as Allah has said,

يَاأَيُّهَا الَّذِينَ آمَنُوا إِذَا نُودِي لِلصَّلاةِ مِنْ يَوْمِ الْجُمُعَةِ
فَاسْعَوْا إِلَى ذِكْرِ اللَّهِ وَذَرُوا الْبَيْعَ

"O you who believe! When the call is proclaimed to pray on Friday, hasten earnestly to the remembrance of Allah, and leave off business (and trade)" (*al-Jumuah* 9).

It consists of two *rakat*s. It is recommended to make *ghusl* for it and to leave early for it.

Upon Whom is the Friday Prayer Obligatory

[It is obligatory upon] every legally responsible [that is, adult and sane], free, male Muslim who has no valid excuse not to attend it.

The Timing for the Friday Prayer

It is acceptable to perform it before high noon. However, to perform it afterwards is preferable as such is the time that the Prophet (peace be upon him) would usually perform it.

What Number Can Constitute the Friday Prayer

It is constituted by a number that is conventionally called a large gathering.

Conditions for the Validity of the Friday Prayer

There are five conditions for the validity of the Friday Prayer:

(1) The proper time.

(2) The intention.

(3) Its occurrence while the person is resident [that is, not traveling].

(4) The presence of the conventionally described "large gathering".

(5) Before the prayer, there are to be two speeches (*khutbah*s) comprising praises of Allah, prayers and salutations upon the Messenger of Allah (peace be upon him), recitation of a verse from the Book of Allah and exhortation to fear Allah. This is to be said aloud so at least the appropriate number of attendees can hear it. It is forbidden to speak while the Imam is delivering his speech. It is also forbidden to step over the necks of the people. If one prays the Friday Prayer, it suffices for the *Dhuhr* Prayer. If a person catches just one *rakah* with the Imam[1], he has caught the Friday Prayer. If he catches less than that, he should make the intention to pray the *Dhuhr* Prayer and perform it as four *rakat*s.

Topic Six:

The *Eid* Prayers

The Wisdom Behind Their Legislation

The *Eid* Prayer is one of the outward expressions of the religion and one of the particular characteristics of the

---

[1] That is by catching at least the bowing of the last *rakah* of the Friday Prayer.—JZ

Nation of the Prophet Muhammad (peace be upon him). By it, one fulfills part of the thanks to the Lord for the ability to fast the month of Ramadhaan or make the pilgrimage to the Sacred House of Allah. Furthermore, it contains a call to mutual compassion and mercy among the believers. It is an all-inclusive gathering and a means of purification of the soul.

Its Status

The *Eid* Prayer is a communal obligation. The Prophet (peace be upon him) and the caliphs after him continually performed it. It is an emphasized sunnah upon every male and female Muslim who is resident and not traveling.

Its Conditions

Its conditions are the same as those for the Friday Prayer, except that in the case of the *Eid* Prayer, the two speeches are simply recommended and are performed after the prayer.

Its Timing

[The time for the *Eid* Prayer] is from the time that the sun is over the horizon after sunrise about the length of a spear until high noon. If the people were not aware that it was the Day of *Eid* until after high noon, they should perform the prayer on the following day in its proper time.

How the *Eid* Prayer is Performed

The *Eid* Prayer is two *rakat*s, as Umar said, "The *Eid* of *al-Fitr* [after Ramadhan] and of *al-Adhha* [after the pilgrimage] are two *rakat*s, complete, without any shortcoming, from the tongue of your Prophet. And foiled will be the one who makes up lies [in such matters]." (Recorded by Ahmad).

It is to be prayed before the speech (*khutbah*). In the first *rakah*, one says *"Allaahu akbar,"* six times after the opening *takbeer* and before seeking refuge in Allah. In the second *rakah*, before reciting, one says it five times.

The Place in Which It is to Be Prayed

It is to be prayed out in the open. However, it is permissible to perform it in the mosques if there is some need to do so.

Recommended Acts Related to the *Eid* Prayers

It is recommended to extol Allah's greatness and make remembrance of Allah at all times; this is a type of *dhikr* or remembrance of Allah that is different from that which is specific said after the prayers. It is recommended to make this remembrance aloud during the night preceding the *Eid* Prayers. This is based on Allah's statement,

$$\text{وَلِتُكْمِلُوا الْعِدَّةَ وَلِتُكَبِّرُوا اللَّهَ عَلَى مَا هَدَاكُمْ}$$

"[Allah wants you] to complete the prescribed period, and to glorify Him in all that He has guided you" (*al-Baqarah* 185). Imam Ahmad said, "Ibn Umar used to extol the greatness of Allah during the entire time of the two *Eid*s." As for making remembrance of Allah during the first ten days of *Dhu-l-Hijjah* [the month of the pilgrimage], Allah says,

$$\text{وَيَذْكُرُوا اسْمَ اللَّهِ فِي أَيَّامٍ مَعْلُومَاتٍ}$$

"And celebrate the name of Allah, through the days appointed" (*al-Hajj* 28).

As for the special time for words of remembrance, this is after every obligatory prayer and is only with respect to *Eid al-Adhha*. It begins after the *Fajr* Prayer on the Day of Arafah (the ninth of *Dhu-l-Hijjah*) until the last of the days of *Tashreeq* (the thirteenth of *Dhu-l-Hijjah*).

It is recommended for those who are going to pray to leave early for the prayer. However, the Imam should wait to leave until the time of the prayer. It is also recommended to cleanse oneself before going and to wear one's best clothing. However, the women must make certain not to expose any kind of beautification.

It is recommended to pray the *Eid al-Adhha* Prayer early while delaying the *Eid al-Fitr* Prayer. It is also recommend to eat an odd number of dates before going to the *Eid al-Fitr* Prayer and to refrain from eating on *Eid al-Adhha* until one can eat from his sacrificed animal.

Topic Seven:

The Prayer for Rain (*al-Istisqaa*) and the Eclipse Prayers (*al-Kusoof*)

The Prayer for Rain:

The Wisdom Behind Its Legislation

Allah created humans with a natural inclination to turn towards Him and beseech Him when they are in need. The prayer for rain (*al-istisqaa* الاستسقاء) is a demonstration of that natural tendency in man as the Muslim turns toward his Lord seeking rain in times of need.

Its Meaning

The meaning of the prayer is to seek rain from Allah for the land and for the humans. This is done through prayer, supplication and seeking Allah's forgiveness.

Its Status

The *Istisqaa* prayer is a stressed sunnah. The Messenger of Allah (peace be upon him) performed it and he announced it among the people so that they would come to the place of the prayer to perform the prayer.

Its timing, characteristics and rulings are the same as those for the *Eid* Prayer.

It is recommended for the Imam to announce the prayer some days before it is performed and also to encourage the people to repent from their sins and stop their wrongdoing, and to fast, give charity and stop their quarreling because sins are one of the causes for drought in the same way that acts of obedience are a cause for blessings and good things.

The Prayer of the Eclipse (*al-Kusoof*):

The Meaning of *al-Kusoof* and the Wisdom Behind the Prayer

The *kusoof* (كسوف) applies to either a full or partial solar or lunar eclipse, wherein a portion or all of the sun's or moon's light are blocked. These events are from the signs of Allah that should encourage people to prepare for the Hereafter and to realize Allah's watchfulness over them. It should lead them to turn to Him under all circumstances and to think about the greatness of His excellence in His creation. It should make the person realize that He alone is worthy of worship.

If there is a solar or lunar eclipse, it is sunnah to perform the eclipse prayer in congregation. Allah has said,

$$ وَمِنْ آيَاتِهِ اللَّيْلُ وَالنَّهَارُ وَالشَّمْسُ وَالْقَمَرُ لَا تَسْجُدُوا لِلشَّمْسِ وَلَا لِلْقَمَرِ وَاسْجُدُوا لِلَّهِ الَّذِي خَلَقَهُنَّ إِنْ كُنْتُمْ إِيَّاهُ تَعْبُدُونَ $$

"Among His signs are the night and the day, and the sun and the moon. Prostrate not to the sun and the moon, but prostrate to Allah, Who created them, if it is [truly] Him you worship" (*Fussilat* 37).

The timing for this prayer is from the beginning of the eclipse until it is finished. It is not to be made up later if one misses it and it is not moved to another time after its time has passed.

The manner in which it is to be prayed is as follows: The prayer consists of two *rakat*s. In the first *rakat*, soorah al-Faatihah is to be recited aloud [by the Imam] followed by a lengthy *soorah* and then a lengthy bow. Then they come up from bowing and say, "*Sami-Allaah liman hamidah*," and, "*Rabanaa lakal-hamd*," and then *soorah al-Faatihah* is recited again followed by another lengthy *soorah*. Then one bows again and comes up and then one makes two long prostrations. The second *rakah* is performed in the same fashion as the first. This is the minimum of the prayer in all of its circumstances. It has other descriptions but this is the most confirmed. If a person performs three acts of bowing or four or five, there is no harm in that if there were some need to do so.

Topic Eight:
The Funeral Prayer

No matter how long a person may live, he must at one time die and move on from the world of deeds to the world of recompense. It is from the rights of a Muslim upon another Muslim that he visits him when he is ill and he follows his funeral procession after he dies. It is also recommended upon visiting the ill that one reminds them to repent and to make a will.

It is also recommended to turn the one who is about to die toward the *qiblah* by turning him on his right side with his face in the direction of the *qiblah* if that is not a hardship upon him. If that is not easy to do, one should put him on his back with his feet toward the *qiblah* and his head elevated a little, so that he may be facing the *qiblah*.[1] Then he should be encouraged to say, "*La ilaaha illa-llah* (There is none worthy of worship except Allah)." His throat should be moistened with water or some kind of drink. *Soorah Ya Seen* should be recited in his presence.[2]

When a Muslim dies, it is recommended to close his eyes, the lower jaw is then to be bound to the head, the joints should be gently flexed; he should be raised from the earth; his clothes should be removed, his private parts should be covered and he should be placed on a bed [or platform] and washed while he is facing the *qiblah* on his right side, if that is easy to do— otherwise he should be placed on his back with his legs extending toward the *qiblah*.

---

[1] There seems to be no authentic sunnah regarding turning the dying person's body toward the *qiblah*. Allah knows best.—JZ

[2] Again, there seems to be no authentic hadith (although there is a weak one) concerning the reciting of this particular *soorah* when a person is about to die. Allah knows best.—JZ

Washing the Deceased

The preferred person to wash the deceased is the one whom he had named in a bequest and then his father, then his grandfather and then his close relative. For the woman, it is the one she had named in a bequest followed by her mother and then her grandmother and then her close female relatives. Each Muslim spouse may wash his or her partner. The one who does the washing must be trustworthy and knowledgeable of the rules of washing.

It is forbidden for a Muslim to wash or bury a non-Muslim. Instead, he should just cover the non-Muslim with soil if there is no one to do a proper burial.

Description of the Recommended Way to Wash the Deceased

When one is going to wash a deceased, he should cover the private parts of the deceased. Then he should raise the head close to how it would be if he were sitting up. Then he should gently press down on his stomach. He should use a lot of water on the body. Then he should wrap a cloth around his hand and clean off the body [disposing of that cloth afterwards]. Then it is preferred to wash him again with a new piece of cloth around the hand. Then he should have the intention to wash the deceased. He mentions the name of Allah and washes the body with water and lote tree leaves or soap. He begins with the body's head and beard. Then he does the right side followed by the left side. Then he washes him a second or third time like the first time. If the body does not become clean, he may continue to wash him until it is cleansed. On the last washing, in addition to water, he uses some type of perfume or camphor. If the person's moustache or fingernails or toenails were long, they should be shortened. Then he should be dried with a cloth. In the case of a woman, her hair should be plaited in three braids and placed to the back.

Shrouding the Deceased

It is recommended to shroud the body in three white sheets that were scented with incense. They are spread out, one over the other. Some perfume is placed in between the different sheets. Then the deceased is laid, stretched out, upon the three sheets. Cotton is placed between the private parts and above it, a garment is tied, acting like short pants, to cover the private parts. That and the rest of the body is then to be perfumed. The uppermost sheet is then folded from the left top side over the right side and then the right side is folded over the left side. The same is then done for the next sheet and then the bottom sheet. The remainders should be tied above the person's head lengthwise, and will be untied at the grave. A young child is shrouded in one garment, although it is also allowed to do so in three garments.

The woman is covered with a loin cloth and then a sleeveless body length shirt and then a headcovering and then two sheets. A young girl is shrouded in a long sleeveless shirt and two sheets.

It is sufficient [that is, not forbidden] to wash the deceased once, covering the whole body, regardless of whether it be a man or a woman. It is also sufficient to shroud the entire body with one garment, again regardless if it be a man or woman.

If a fetus reaches the age of at least four months and is then aborted and dies, it is to be washed and prayed over.

Description of the Prayer Over the Deceased

It is the sunnah for the Imam to stand level with the chest of the deceased if it is a male and level to the middle of the body if it is a female. He makes four *takbeer*s (statements of "*Allaahu akbar*"), raising the hands each time. After the first *takbeer*, he seeks refuge in Allah from Satan, he recites, "*Bismilaahi-rrahmani-rraheem* (In the name of Allah, the Beneficent, the Merciful)," and then he recites *soorah al-Faatihah*. However, he does not make any opening supplication.

After the second *takbeer*, he says,

اللَّهُمَّ صَلِّ عَلَى مُحَمَّدٍ وَعَلَى آلِ مُحَمَّدٍ كَمَا صَلَّيْتَ عَلَى
إِبْرَاهِيمَ وَعَلَى آلِ إِبْرَاهِيمَ إِنَّكَ حَمِيدٌ مَجِيدٌ اللَّهُمَّ بَارِكْ عَلَى
مُحَمَّدٍ وَعَلَى آلِ مُحَمَّدٍ كَمَا بَارَكْتَ عَلَى إِبْرَاهِيمَ وَعَلَى آلِ
إِبْرَاهِيمَ إِنَّكَ حَمِيدٌ مَجِيدٌ

Allaahumma salli ala muhammadin wa ala aali muhammadin kama salaita ala ibraaheem wa ala aali ibraheem innaka hameedun majeed. Wa baarik ala muhammadin wa ala aali muhammadin kama barakta ala ibraaheema wa ala aali ibraaheema innaka hameedun majeed (O Allah, grace Muhammad and the family of Muhammad as You graced Abraham and the family of Abraham, for verily You are praiseworthy, exalted. And bless Muhammad and the family of Muhammad as You blessed Abraham and the family of Abraham, for verily You are praiseworthy, exalted).

Then he makes a third *takbeer* followed by this supplication:

اللَّهُمَّ اغْفِرْ لِحَيِّنَا وَمَيِّتِنَا وَشَاهِدِنَا وَغَائِبِنَا وَصَغِيرِنَا وَكَبِيرِنَا
وَذَكَرِنَا وَأُنْثَانَا اللَّهُمَّ مَنْ أَحْيَيْتَهُ مِنَّا فَأَحْيِهِ عَلَى الإِسْلاَم وَمَنْ
تَوَفَّيْتَهُ مِنَّا فَتَوَفَّهُ عَلَى الإِيمَان اللَّهُمَّ اغْفِرْ لَهُ وَارْحَمْهُ وَاعْفُ
عَنْهُ وَعَافِهِ وَأَكْرِمْ نُزُلَهُ وَوَسِّعْ مُدْخَلَهُ وَاغْسِلْهُ بِالمَاءِ وَالثَّلْجِ
وَالبَرَدِ وَنَقِّهِ مِنَ الْخَطَايَا كَمَا يُنَقَّى الثَّوْبُ الأَبْيَضُ مِنَ الدَّنَسِ
وَأَبْدِلْهُ دَارًا خَيْرًا مِنْ دَارِهِ وَأَهْلاً خَيْرًا مِنْ أَهْلِهِ وَزَوْجًا خَيْرًا
مِنْ زَوْجِهِ وَقِهِ عَذَابَ الْقَبْرِ وَعَذَابَ النَّارِ

Allahumma-ghfir lihayyinaa wa mayyitinaa wa shaahidina wa ghaa-ibinaa wa sagheerina wa kabeerina wa dhakarinaa wa unthaanaa. Allahumma man ahyaitahu minna fa-ahyihi ala-l-islaam wa man tawaffaitahu minnaa fatawaffahu ala-l-eemaan. Allahumma-ghfir lahu wa-rhamhu wa-'fu anhu wa aafihi wa akram nuzulahu wa wassi mudkhalahu wa-ghsilhu bi-l-ma-i wa-l-thalji wa-l-baradi wa naqqihu min al-khataayaa kamaa yunaqqa-thaubu-l-abyadhu mina-danas wa abdilhu daaran khairan min daarihi wa ahlan khairan min ahlihi wa zaujan khairan min zaujihi waqihi adhaaba-l-qabri wa adhaaba-naar. (O Allah, forgive our living and our dead, our present and our absent, our young and our old, our males and our females. O Allah, for the one You continue to give life among us, keep him alive in Islam. And for the one that You give death among us, let him die in faith. O Allah, forgive him, have mercy on him, pardon him and make him safe and make his resting place an honorable one and make his entry way expansive. Clean him with the water, snow and hail and purify him from sins like a white garment is cleansed from dirt. Replace for him an abode which is better than his abode [here] and a family that is better than his family and a spouse that is better than his spouse. Save him from the punishment of the grave and the punishment of the fire.)

If the deceased is a youngster, then after saying, "O Allah, for the one You continue to give life among us, keep him alive in Islam. And for the one that You give death among us, let him die in faith," one should say,

اللهم اجعله ذخراً لوالديه وفرطاً و شفيعاً مجاباً اللهم ثقّل به موازينهما وأعظم به أجورهما وألحقه بصالح سلف المؤمنين واجعله في كفالة إبراهيم وقه برحمتك عذاب الجحيم

Allahumma-jalhu dhakhiran li-waalidaihi wa faratan wa shafeean mujaaban. Allahumma thaqqil bihi mawaazeenahuma wa adham bihi ujoorahumaa wa alhaqahu bisaalih salafi-l-mumineen wajalhu fi kafaalah ibraaheem waqihu birahmatika adhaaba-l-jaheem (O Allah, make him a stored treasure for his parents and a predecessor and a responded to intercessor. O Allah, make their scales heavy because of him and make their rewards greater. Join him with the pious, preceding believers. And place him under the protection of Abraham and save him, by Your mercy, from the punishment of the Fire.)

Then the person makes the fourth *takbeer*, waits a little and then gives one salutation to his right.

The Virtue of Praying the Prayer Over the Deceased

The one who prays over the deceased will receive a *qeeraat* of reward and a *qeeraat* is equivalent in size to the Mountain of Uhud. If the person then follows the funeral procession until the burial, he will receive two *qeeraat*s as a reward.

It is recommended for four people to carry the deceased. It is recommended to walk quickly to the burial ground. It is best for those walking accompanying the procession to walk in front of the deceased while those who are riding animals should be behind the procession.

Description of the Grave and Burial and What is Prohibited at the Gravesites

The grave must be dug deep. At the bottom of the grave, a section is dug out [horizontally] toward the *qiblah* in which the deceased is going to be placed. This is known as *lahad* and is considered preferable to *shaq* [wherein the body is simply laid at the bottom of the open trench and not in a side opening]. The one who is putting the body in the grave should say, "*Bismilaahi ala millati rasoolilaah* (In the name of Allah, upon the way of the messenger of Allah)." The body is placed into the insert upon its right side, facing the *qiblah*. [The covering over the head should now be untied.] A layer of wood or big stones is then placed over the body. The body is then buried and the grave is raised only a handspan above the ground level. It is then sprinkled over with water.

It is forbidden to build anything upon the grave, plaster the grave, walk upon it, pray at it, take it as a mosque, seek blessings from it or wipe it for blessings, put candles upon it or circumambulate it.

It is recommended to prepare food for the family of the deceased and to take it to them. It is disliked for the family of the deceased to prepare food for the people.

It is recommended for the one visiting the graves to say, "Peace be upon you, abode of believers. Allah willing, we will be joining you. May Allah have mercy on the earlier and later ones among you. We ask Allah for ourselves and yourselves well-being. O Allah, do not forbid us from their reward and do not put us to trial after them. Forgive us and them."

It is also encouraged to give condolences to those affected by the death, before or after the burial, up to three days and nights, unless someone is not present [in which case one may pay him condolences later].

The one who is afflicted with a calamity should say, "We belong to Allah and unto Allah we shall return. O Allah reward me for my hardship and leave one better than it for me."

It is permissible to cry over somebody's death. However, it is forbidden [to get so frantic and upset] that one tears one's clothing, strikes one's cheeks or wails and so on.

Chapter Three:
Zakaat

ˈThis chapter comprises an introduction and two subsections, one on the general rules of *zakaat* and the second on *zakaat al-fitr*.

Introduction

The Wisdom of Legislating *Zakaat*

The wisdom behind the legislation of *zakaat* includes the following:

(1) It purifies the souls of humans from the depravity of miserliness and stinginess and their evils.

(2) It comforts and assists the poor and helps the needy and destitute fulfill some of their needs.

(3) It establishes the general welfare upon which the life and well-being of the society rests.

(4) It limits the growth of wealth among the rich and in the hands of the merchants and professionals, such that wealth is not restricted to certain classes and such that wealth is not circulated only among the rich.

The Definition of *Zakaat*

Zakaat (زكاة) is the obligatory amount that one must give out, to its rightful recipients, of the wealth that has met a specific minimum and special conditions. It is a cleansing of the person and a purification of his soul. Allah has said,

$$خُذْ مِنْ أَمْوَالِهِمْ صَدَقَةً تُطَهِّرُهُمْ وَتُزَكِّيهِمْ بِهَا$$

"Of their goods take alms, so that you may purify and sanctify them" (*al-Taubah* 68).

The Place of *Zakaat* in Islam

It is one of the five pillars of Islam. It has been mentioned in connection with prayers in numerous places in the Book of Allah.

The Status of *Zakaat*

Zakaat is an obligation from Allah upon every Muslim who possesses the minimum amount of wealth given certain conditions. Allah has obligated it in His book and the Prophet (peace be upon him) used to take it from the people. He ordered that it be taken from whomever it was obligatory upon, whether old or young, male or female, healthy, ill or insane. Allah says,

$$خُذْ مِنْ أَمْوَالِهِمْ صَدَقَةً تُطَهِّرُهُمْ وَتُزَكِّيهِمْ بِهَا$$

"Of their goods take alms, that you may purify and sanctify them thereby" (*al-Taubah* 68). Allah also says,

$$يَاأَيُّهَا الَّذِينَ آمَنُوا أَنفِقُوا مِنْ طَيِّبَاتِ مَا كَسَبْتُمْ وَمِمَّا$$

$$أَخْرَجْنَا لَكُمْ مِنَ الأَرْضِ$$

"O you who believe! Give of the good things which you have earned, and of the fruits of the earth which We have produced for you" (*al-Baqarah* 267). Again, Allah says,

وَأَقِيمُوا الصَّلَاةَ وَآتُوا الزَّكَاةَ

"Establish the prayers and give the *zakaat*" (*al-Muzzammil* 20).

The Messenger of Allah (peace be upon him) said,

بُنِيَ الإِسْلَامُ عَلَى خَمْسٍ شَهَادَةِ أَنْ لَا إِلَهَ إِلا اللَّهُ وَأَنَّ مُحَمَّدًا
رَسُولُ اللَّهِ وَإِقَامِ الصَّلَاةِ وَإِيتَاءِ الزَّكَاةِ وَالْحَجِّ الْبَيْتِ وَصَوْمِ
رَمَضَانَ

"Islam is built upon five [pillars]: testifying that there is none worthy of worship except Allah and that Muhammad is the Messenger of Allah, establishing the prayers, giving the zakaat, making the pilgrimage to the House and fasting the month of Ramadhaan." (Recorded by al-Bukhari and Muslim.)

Topic One:
Some Rules Concerning *Zakaat*

The Types of Wealth Upon Which Zakaat is Obligatory

[*Zakaat* is obligatory upon] monetary assets, livestock, agricultural produce and merchandise goods. [Each category is discussed separately below.]

(1) The Zakaat on Monetary Assets: Gold, Silver and Currency

Zakaat of 2.5% is obligatory upon gold if the amount of gold one owns reaches twenty *mithqaal*.[1]

Zakaat of 2.5% is obligatory upon silver if the amount of silver one owns reaches two hundred *dirham*s.

Paper currency is considered according to its value. If the paper currency reaches the equivalent of the *nisaab*[2] of either gold or silver, *zakaat* becomes obligatory upon it. Once again, the amount of *zakaat* will be 2.5%, given that the wealth was with the person for an entire year.

Note that it is forbidden for men to wear gold; however, they may wear a silver ring or have silver embroidery on the swords and so forth.

(2) The Zakaat on Livestock

Zakaat is obligatory on camels, cattle and sheep/goats if they are tended to for a year or more, freely grazing in pastures or vacant, open lands. If their amounts reach the *nisaab* and are in one's possession for a whole year, one pays *zakaat* on them if they were held for the purpose of milking and reproduction.

The following table shows the amounts to be paid in the case of sheep or goats [with forty being the minimum or *nisaab* below which one is not required to pay anything]:

---

[1] Each *mithqaal* is equivalent to about four grams.

[2] The *nisaab* is the minimum amount [of gold or silver] that requires one to pay *zakaat*.

Number of Sheep/Goats	Zakaat
40 to 120	One sheep
121 to 200	Two sheep
201 to 300	Three sheep
For every additional 100	One additional sheep

The following table shows the amounts to be paid in the case of cattle [with thirty being the minimum or *nisaab* below which one is not required to pay anything]:

Number of Cattle	Zakaat
30 to 39	A young bull or young cow, one year old
40 to 59	A young cow, two years old
60	Two young, one year old cows
For an additional 30	A young, one year old cow
For an additional 40	A young, two year old cow

The following table shows the amounts to be paid in the case of camels [with five being the minimum or *nisaab* below which one is not required to pay anything]:

Number of Camels	Zakaat
5 to 9	A sheep
10 to 14	Two sheep
15 to 19	Three sheep
20 to 24	Four sheep
25 to 35	A she-camel which is a year old
36 to 45	A she-camel which is two years old
46 to 60	A she-camel which is three years old
61 to 75	A four year old camel
76 to 90	Two young she-camels
91 to 120	Two three year old camels
121	Three young she-camels; for every additional forty, a young she-camel is due; for every additional fifty, a three year old she-camel is due

If the livestock (camels, cattle and sheep) are for the purpose of trade and investment and they are owned for one year, then 2.5% of their value will be given as *zakaat*. If they are not for trade, there is no such zakaat on them.

When paying *zakaat*, only female animals are acceptable. A male is not sufficient except in the case of cattle or when given a camel which is a year or two or three years old instead of a she-camel or if all of the livestock are male.

Zakaat on Agricultural Produce

Zakaat is obligatory upon all grains and all produce that are measured by dry volume and stored, such as dates and raisins. The *nisaab* is three hundred *saa* or approximately 624 kilograms.

Different varieties of the same produce, such as different types of dates, will be weighed together to reach the *nisaab*.

What is Obligatory Concerning Grains and Produce

(1) One tenth (*al-ushr*) of the produce is to be given from the produce of land that is naturally irrigated, such as by rainwater only.

(2) One twentieth is to be given from the produce of the land that is irrigated by man-engineered means, such as by water from canals [and so forth].

(3) Three quarters of one tenth is to be given if the produce was partially irrigated naturally and partially irrigated by man-engineered means.

There is no zakaat on vegetables and fruits if they are for the purpose of trade. However, 2.5% of their value is given if they reach the level of the *nisaab* and are in one's possession for one year.

What is derived from the sea, such as pearls, rubies and fish, have no *zakaat* on them. However, if they are kept for trade purposes, 2.5% of their value is to be paid if they reach the *nisaab* and are in one's possession for an entire year.

Al-rikaaz refers to buried treasures in the earth. It is obligatory to give one-fifth of that (*al-khums*), regardless of whether it be a large or small amount. This money is to be given to the same categories of those who receive the *fai* (wealth taken from an enemy with no fighting). The remaining four-fifths goes to the person who found the treasure.

Zakaat on Merchandise Goods

Merchandise goods are those that are kept for the purpose of buying and selling in order to make a profit, whether they be immovable property, food, drink, utensils and so forth.

If the value of the merchandise goods reaches the *nisaab* [of monetary assets] and if the goods are in one's possession for one year, then *zakaat* becomes obligatory upon them. 2.5% of the total value is to be given. It is permissible to give 2.5% of the actual goods themselves as *zakaat*.

If the person who holds such goods intends simply to possess them and not deal in business with them, there is no zakaat on them.

The payments for a share or profits from trade have zakaat on them if the original principle has been in the person's possession for a year and the amounts reach the *nisaab*.

The Conditions for the Obligation of Zakaat

Zakaat is obligatory upon every free Muslim who possesses the *nisaab* with a complete and independent ownership and the property is in his possession for one year, except in the case of the *ushr* [payment made on produce].

Paying the Zakaat:

The Time for Paying the Zakaat

One must give the zakaat immediately when it becomes due, which is the same ruling for oaths and expiations. This is because an imperative that has not been restricted in any way implies immediate response, and Allah has said [in the imperative],

$$وَآتُوا الزَّكَاةَ$$

"Give the *zakaat*" (*al-Muzzammil* 20).

He may delay its payment until a time it is needed or for a near relative or neighbor.

The Ruling Concerning Withholding Zakaat

Whoever denies the obligation of zakaat, knowingly and intentionally, has committed an act of disbelief, even if he pays the zakaat. This is because he has belied Allah, His Messenger and the consensus of the Muslim community. He is to be asked to repent. If he repents, [that is good]; if not, he is to be killed [as an apostate]. If a person withholds the zakaat out of greed or being lackadaisical, it is to be taken from him and he is to be punished due to the sin he has committed.

The guardians of the young or insane are to pay the zakaat on their behalf.

Recommended Acts When Paying Zakaat

(1) One should pay the zakaat openly so that he would be free of any suspicion.

(2) One should distribute it himself to ensure that it gets to its rightful recipients.

(3) Upon paying it, one should say, "O Allah, make it a beneficial gain and do not make it a loss."

(4) The one who receives the zakaat should say, "May Allah reward you for what you have given and bless you in what remains [with you] and make it purifying for you."

(5) It is recommended to give it to poor relatives for whom one is not financially responsible.

The Recipients of Zakaat

The groups of people to whom one is allowed to give zakaat are eight. They are the ones mentioned in Allah's statement,

إِنَّمَا الصَّدَقَاتُ لِلْفُقَرَاءِ وَالْمَسَاكِينِ وَالْعَامِلِينَ عَلَيْهَا وَالْمُؤَلَّفَةِ قُلُوبُهُمْ وَفِي الرِّقَابِ وَالْغَارِمِينَ وَفِي سَبِيلِ اللّهِ وَابْنِ السَّبِيلِ فَرِيضَةً مِنْ اللّهِ وَاللّهُ عَلِيمٌ حَكِيمٌ

"Alms are for the poor and the needy, and those employed to administer the (funds); for those whose hearts are to be reconciled (to the truth); for those in bondage and in debt; in the cause of Allah; and for the wayfarer: (thus is it) ordained by Allah, and Allah is full of knowledge and wisdom" (al-Taubah 60).

Hence, they are as follows:

(1) The poor: those who cannot meet some of their basic needs.

(2) The needy: those who meet most or half of their basic needs.

(3) Those employed to administer the funds: those who collect and watch over the funds— but this is only if they do not receive a wage.

(4) Those whose hearts are to be reconciled to the truth: those leaders of their people who one hopes will embrace Islam or those who are to be given to repel their harm or by giving to them one hopes to strengthen their faith or have someone similar embrace Islam.

(5) Those in bondage: those slaves who have made agreements with their masters to pay for their freedom.

(6) Those in debt— this group falls into two categories: (a) those who have incurred a debt to reconcile opposing parties and (b) a person himself who has fallen into debt and does not have the means to repay it.

(7) In the cause of Allah: to those volunteer fighters striving for the sake of Allah and those calling to the way of Allah and whatever helps and supports their activities.

(8) Wayfarers: those travelers who are cut off from their homeland and do not have wealth with them that will allow them to reach their homes.

Topic Two:
Zakaat al-Fitr

Its Wisdom

[Zakaat al-Fitr is the zakaat that is paid at the end of the month of Ramadhaan.] Its wisdom includes purifying the fasting person from his associated acts of useless and foul speech [during his fasting]. Furthermore, it enriches the poor and needy and therefore makes it such that they do not have to beg on the Day of Eid.

Its Amount and the Types of Foods in Which it is to Be Given

The amount to be given as *zakaat al-fitr* is one *saa*, a *saa* is four *mudd*, which is approximately equal to three kilograms. It is to be paid in what is normally considered the staple food of the land, whether it be barley, dates, rice, dried yogurt and so forth.

The Time of Its Obligation and the Time of Its Payment

The obligation to [definitely] pay zakaat al-fitr comes about by the presence of the night before the Eid. However, it may also be paid one or two days before the day of Eid. Ibn Umar used to do that. A virtuous time to pay it is after sunrise on the Day of Eid, just before the prayer; this is because the Prophet (peace be upon him) ordered the people to give their zakaat al-fitr before leaving for the prayer.

Upon Whom is Zakaat al-Fitr Obligatory

Zakaat al-Fitr is obligatory upon every free or slave Muslim, male or female, young or old who has staple food more than what he needs for his day and night. It is also recommended to pay it on behalf of the fetus in the womb of its mother.

The Recipients of Zakaat al-Fitr

The recipients of zakaat al-fitr are the same as those for the general zakaat, except that the poor and needy are more deserving of this zakaat because the Prophet (peace be upon him) said,

أغنوهم عن السؤال هذا اليوم

"Enrich them such that they will not have to beg on this day."[1]

---

[1] Al-Albaani has discussed the different chains and wordings of this hadith and has concluded that it is a weak hadith. See Muhammad Naasir al-Deen al-Albaani, *Irwa al-Ghaleel fi Takhreej Ahaadeeth Manaar al-Sabeel* (Beirut: al-Maktab al-Islaami, 1979), vol. 3, pp. 332-334.

Chapter Four:
The Fast

This chapter is comprised of an introduction and the following four topics:

Topic One: The conditions for the fast;

Topic Two: Acceptable excuses to break the fast;

Topic Three: What is recommended, disliked or forbidden during the fast;

Topic Four: *Itikaaf*.

Introduction

Definition of Fasting

Lexically, *al-saum* (الصــوم) means to refrain from something. Legally speaking, it refers to refraining, with the intention of worship, from food, drink, sexual intercourse and other acts that break the fast from dawn until sunset.

The History of the Obligation of Fasting

Allah obligated the fast for the Nation of Muhammad (peace be upon him) in the same way that He obligated it for the previous peoples. Allah says,

يَاأَيُّهَا الَّذِينَ آمَنُوا كُتِبَ عَلَيْكُمُ الصِّيَامُ كَمَا كُتِبَ عَلَى
الَّذِينَ مِنْ قَبْلِكُمْ لَعَلَّكُمْ تَتَّقُونَ

"O you who believe! Fasting is prescribed for you as it was prescribed for those before you, that you may attain *taqwa* (fear of Allah)" (*al-Baqarah* 183). That obligation began in the month of Shabaan in the second year after the Hijrah.

The Benefits of Fasting

Fasting has spiritual, societal and health benefits. The spiritual benefits include the practicing and strengthening of one's patience, knowing how to control oneself and help oneself in that realm. The soul finds within itself the ability to have *taqwa* and to improve upon it.

Societal benefits include the fact that it adds a certain system and unity to the society, engenders love for justice and equity, brings about mercy and compassion among the believers as well as good behavior. Furthermore, it keeps the society from evil and wickedness.

Health benefits include the purifying of the intestine, improving the health of the stomach, cleansing the body of impurities, decreasing the level of fat in the body and decreasing the heaviness of the stomach due to fat.

Confirming the Beginning of the Month of Ramadhaan

The beginning of the month of Ramadhaan is confirmed by one of two means: First, the previous month, Shabaan, is completed. In other words, if Shabaan finishes thirty days, the thirty-first day will definitely be the beginning of the month of Ramadhaan.

Second, the new moon is seen. If the crescent of the month of Ramadhaan is seen on the night before [what would be] the thirtieth of Shabaan, then the month of Ramadhaan has begun and it is obligatory to fast. Allah says,

فَمَنْ شَهِدَ مِنكُمُ الشَّهْرَ فَلْيَصُمْهُ

"Whoever is present [that is, not travelling] among you during the month shall fast" (*al-Baqarah* 185).

The Messenger of Allah (peace be upon him) said,

إِذَا رَأَيْتُمُ الْهِلَالَ فَصُومُوا وَإِذَا رَأَيْتُمُوهُ فَأَفْطِرُوا فَإِنْ غُمَّ عَلَيْكُمْ فَصُومُوا ثَلَاثِينَ يَوْمًا

"If you see the crescent, fast. And if you see it [at the end of the month], break your fast. If it is obscured to you, then fast thirty days." (Recorded by Muslim.)

If a people of a certain land see the crescent, they must fast. However, the birth or appearance of the moon will be different for different places. The birth in Asia is different from the birth in Europe and its birth in Africa is different than its birth in America, for example. Based on that, every country or locale will have its own ruling. But if all of the Muslims throughout the earth fast according to one sighting, that will be from the beautiful aspects of Islam and a sign of affection, oneness and brotherhood.

For the beginning of Ramadhaan, the testimony of one just person is sufficient or two just people as the Messenger of Allah (peace be upon him) accepted the testimony of one person concerning his sighting of the crescent of Ramadhaan. (Recorded by Muslim.) However, for the sighting of the moon of Shawaal to break the fast, this is not confirmed except by the testimony of two just witnesses, as the Messenger of Allah (peace be upon him) did not allow the witness of only one just person for the breaking of the fast. (Recorded by Muslim.)

The Obligation of Fasting Ramadhaan

Fasting the month of Ramadhaan is obligatory according to the Book of Allah, the sunnah and consensus of the community. It is one of the five pillars of Islam. Allah has said,

شَهْرُ رَمَضَانَ الَّذِي أُنزِلَ فِيهِ الْقُرْآنُ هُدًى لِلنَّاسِ وَبَيِّنَاتٍ مِنْ الْهُدَى وَالْفُرْقَانِ فَمَنْ شَهِدَ مِنْكُمْ الشَّهْرَ فَلْيَصُمْهُ

"Ramadhaan is the (month) in which was sent down the Quran, as a guide to mankind, also clear (signs) for guidance and judgment (between right and wrong). So every one of you who is present (at his home) during that month should spend it in fasting" (*al-Baqarah* 185). And the Messenger of Allah (peace be upon him) said,

بُنِيَ الإِسْلامُ عَلَى خَمْسٍ شَهَادَةِ أَنْ لا إِلَهَ إِلا اللَّهُ وَأَنَّ مُحَمَّدًا رَسُولُ اللَّهِ وَإِقَامِ الصَّلاةِ وَإِيتَاءِ الزَّكَاةِ وَالْحَجِّ الْبَيْتِ وَصَوْمِ رَمَضَانَ

"Islam is built upon five [pillars]: testifying that there is none worthy of worship except Allah and that Muhammad is the Messenger of Allah, establishing the prayers, giving the zakaat, making the pilgrimage to the House and fasting the month of Ramadhaan." (Recorded by al-Bukhari and Muslim.)

Topic One:
Conditions Related to Fasting

The Conditions Requiring One to Fast

[These conditions are the following:]
(1) Being Muslim.
(2) Being adult.
(3) Being sane.
(4) Having the ability to fast.

The Essential Components of the Fast

[The essential components of the fast are:]
(1) The intention: this is the determination of the heart to fast, to implement the command of Allah and to get closer to Allah. The Prophet (peace be upon him) said,

$$إِنَّمَا الأَعْمَالُ بِالنِّيَّاتِ$$

"Surely, all actions are but driven by intentions." (Recorded by al-Bukhari.)
(2) Refraining, meaning staying away, from the things that break the fast, which are eating, drinking and sexual intercourse.
(3) The proper time, that is, the daytime which is from dawn until sunset.

The Conditions for the Soundness of the Fast

[The conditions for the soundness of the fast are as follows:]

(1) Being Muslim.

(2) Having the intention during the nighttime [that is, before the arrival of the dawn of the day in which one is to fast].

(3) Being sane.

(4) Being of the age of discernment.

(5) No menstrual blood flowing.

(6) No post-partum blood flowing, as the soundness of the fast of a woman requires that she be pure of menses or post-partum bleeding.

Recommended Acts of the Fast

(1) Breaking the fast promptly, that is one should break the fast as soon as it is certain that the sun has set.

(2) Breaking the fast by eating fresh or dry dates or drinking water. The preferred of those is the first. It is also preferred to eat them in an odd number, three, five or seven.

(3) Supplication at the time of breaking one's fast. One should say,

$$اللَّهُمَّ لَكَ صُمْتُ وَعَلَى رِزْقِكَ أَفْطَرْتُ فتقبل منا إنك$$

$$السميع العليم$$

"O Allah, for You I have fasted and with sustenance from You do I break my fast. Accept from us [our fasting] for You are the All-Hearing, the All-Knowing." (Recorded by Abu Dawood.[1])

(4) Having *sahoor*, which is the eating and drinking at the end of the night with the intention of fasting the next day.

---

[1] This hadith has a weak chain. See Saleem al-Hilaali, *Saheeh Kitaab al-Adhkaar wa Dhaeefahu* (Madinah: Maktabah al-Ghurabaa al-Athariyyah, 1413 A.H.), vol. 1, p. 495.—JZ

(5) Delaying the *sahoor* until the final portion of the night [just before dawn].

Actions That are Disliked During the Fast

A number of acts are disliked because they may lead the person to do something that will ruin his fast, even though they in themselves do not break the fast. These are the following acts:

(1) Putting water well into the mouth and throat while rinsing as part of ablution.

(2) Kissing, as it sparks the desires that may lead one to break the fast by ejaculating or sexual intercourse, wherein one will have to atone for the act.

(3) Continually looking at one's spouse with desire.

(4) Thinking about sexual intercourse.

(5) Touching a woman with one's hand or touching her with one's body.

Topic Two:

Acceptable Excuses to Not Fast

(1) A woman on her menses or with post-partum bleeding is required to break her fast.

(2) A person who is needed to rescue another Muslim from death, such as drowning and so forth, [may break his or her fast].

(3) A traveler is permitted to shorten his prayers and it is sunnah for him to break his fast.

(4) An ill person who fears he will be harmed [by fasting may also break his fast].

(5) A traveling person who returns to his home during the daytime.

(6) A pregnant or milking mother [may break the fast] if she fears for herself or her child. If she breaks her fast fearing only for her child, the one financially responsible for her must feed a poor person for every day she did not fast. In either case, she must make up the days of not fasting later.

What Nullifies the Fast

The following acts nullify the fast:

(1) Apostatizing from Islam.

(2) Having the intention and determination to break the fast.

(3) Having doubts about continuing the fast.

(4) Intentionally vomiting.

(5) Anal enemas or intravenous intake of foods.

(6) Menstrual or post-partum bleeding.

(7) Swallowing phlegm if it reaches all the way to the mouth.

(8) Cupping [a medical practice meant to release blood from the body] for both the one being cupped and the one doing the cupping.

(9) Ejaculation of sperm due to repeated looks.

(10) Ejaculation of sperm or release of prostatic fluid due to kissing, touching, masturbation or touching in a manner less than sexual intercourse.

(11) Anything which reaches to the stomach, throat or brain of fluids or other things.

Important Notes

Whoever has sexual intercourse during the daytime of Ramadhaan must make up that day later and atone for his act, if such was done intentionally. If it was done out of forgetfulness, the fast is still valid and he does not have to make up the day later or atone for his deed.

If a woman is forced to have sexual intercourse during the daytime of Ramadhaan or if she were ignorant or forgetful, then her fast is valid. If she were forced into doing that, she must only make the day up later. If she did that act willingly and intentionally, then she must make the day up and atone for her act.

The atonement for such an act is the following: The person must free a slave. If that is not feasible, he or she must fast two consecutive months. If they are not able to do that, they must feed sixty poor people. If they cannot do that, then they are absolved of any specific act of atonement.

If a person has intercourse with his wife but not in her sexual organ, then he must make up that day and repent to Allah [without the act of atonement].

It is recommended to make up the days of Ramadhaan immediately and in successive days. If a person leaves those missed days until the following Ramadhaan without any valid excuse for doing so, he must still make up those days but must in addition feed one poor person for every such day.

If a person dies while still having to perform fasts of an oath or a pilgrimage due to an oath, then his heirs should perform said act on his behalf.

Topic Four:
Itikaaf

Definition

Lexically, *itikaaf* (اعتكاف) implies remaining somewhere, continuance, place and confinement. Legally, it means the staying and remaining in the mosque for the purpose of worship, with a specific intention to perform the act in a specific manner.

The Wisdom Behind Its Being Sanctioned

Itikaaf allows the heart to be free of the affairs of the world and to concentrate itself upon the worship of Allah and His remembrance.

By this act, the soul submits itself to its Lord and turns over its affairs to Allah and stands at the door to His grace and mercy.

The Types of *Itikaaf*

Itikaaf is of two types:

(1) The obligatory *itikaaf*: This is the result of a vow that a person makes. For example, one might say, "If I am successful in that deed, I shall spend three days in *itikaaf*," or, "If this is made easy for me, I shall spend such and such time in *itikaaf*."

(2) The *itikaaf* which forms part of the emphasized sunnah: The best of this category is to perform *itikaaf* during the last ten days of the month of Ramadhaan.

The Essential Components of *Itikaaf*

(1) The person who is performing the *itikaaf*— *itikaaf* is an action and it requires a "doer".

(2) Remaining in the mosque. Ali said, "There is no *itikaaf* except in a congregational mosque." Furthermore, if the person performing the *itikaaf* does so in a mosque in which the congregational prayers are performed, he would be most ready to perform those prayers in the best manner possible and the most complete manner is by performing them in congregation.

(3) The place where one actually stays: this is the place that the person takes as his "residence" as such during his *itikaaf*.

The Conditions for the Soundness of the *Itikaaf*

(1) The person performing the *itikaaf* must be a Muslim; it is not valid from a disbeliever.

(2) He must be a person of discernment; it is not valid from an insane person or a young child.

(3) It must be performed in a mosque in which the congregational prayers are held, at least with respect to men such is the case.

(4) The one performing the *itikaaf* must be free of sexual defilement, menses and post-partum bleeding.

The *Itikaaf* is Voided by the Following Acts

(1) Sexual intercourse, even if without ejaculation, as Allah has said,

وَلَا تُبَاشِرُوهُنَّ وَأَنْتُمْ عَاكِفُونَ فِي الْمَسَاجِدِ

"Do not associate with your wives while you are making *itikaaf* in the mosques" (*al-Baqarah* 187).

(2) Instigating sexual intercourse.

(3) Falling unconscious or becoming insane, regardless if it be through intoxicants or otherwise.

(4) Apostatizing from Islam.

(5) Leaving the mosque for no valid reason.

Excuses That Permit One to Leave the Mosque

The excuses that permit the one performing *itikaaf* to leave the mosque are of three varieties:

(1) Legal excuses: This would include going out for the Friday Prayer or the two Eid Prayers if the mosque in which he was performing *itikaaf* does not have the Friday or Eid Prayers. The reason for this excuse is that *itikaaf* is considered an act taking one closer to Allah by avoiding sins and fleeing from them; however, not performing the Friday or Eid Prayers are sins that go against the notion of getting closer to Allah by *itikaaf*.

(2) Natural excuses: These would include the need to urinate and defecate or wash oneself after a wet dream if one could not do that washing in the mosque itself. However, these acts are conditional upon the person not remaining outside the mosque more than the time that he needs to perform those acts.

(3) Excuses of a necessary nature: These would include a person fearing that his wealth will be lost or fearing for his possessions or he fears for his own life or harm if he were to remain in the mosque in a state of *itikaaf*.

Chapter Five: Hajj [Pilgrimage] and Umrah [Lesser Visitation]

This chapter is comprised of an introduction and the following six topics:

Topic One: The conditions for the hajj and umrah;

Topic Two: The essential aspects of the hajj and umrah;

Topic Three: The obligatory acts of the hajj and umrah;

Topic Four: Forbidden acts while in the inviolable state of pilgrimage;

Topic Five: Sites for entering the inviolable state of pilgrimage;

Topic Six: The sacrifice and *aqeeqah*.

Introduction

The Place of the Pilgrimage in Islam

The pilgrimage is the fifth pillar of the five pillars of Islam. It was made obligatory in the ninth year after the Hijrah.

Allah says,

وَلِلَّهِ عَلَى النَّاسِ حِجُّ الْبَيْتِ مَنِ اسْتَطَاعَ إِلَيْهِ سَبِيلاً

"Pilgrimage is a duty mankind owes to Allah, those who can afford the journey" (ali-Imraan 97). The Messenger of Allah (peace be upon him) said,

$$\text{بُنِيَ الإِسْلامُ عَلَى خَمْسٍ شَهَادَةِ أَنْ لا إِلَهَ إِلا اللَّهُ وَأَنَّ مُحَمَّدًا}$$
$$\text{رَسُولُ اللَّهِ وَإِقَامِ الصَّلاةِ وَإِيتَاءِ الزَّكَاةِ وَالْحَجِّ الْبَيْتِ وَصَوْمِ}$$
$$\text{رَمَضَانَ}$$

"Islam is built upon five [pillars]: testifying that there is none worthy of worship except Allah and that Muhammad is the Messenger of Allah, establishing the prayers, giving the zakaat, making the pilgrimage to the House and fasting the month of Ramadhaan." (Recorded by al-Bukhari and Muslim.)

The Legal Status of the Pilgrimage

The pilgrimage is an obligation from Allah upon His servants, to be performed at least once in one's lifetime. The Prophet (peace be upon him) said,

$$\text{الْحَجُّ مَرَّةٌ فَمَنْ زَادَ فَهُوَ تَطَوُّعٌ}$$

"The pilgrimage [need only be done] once. Whoever does more, it is done voluntarily."[1]

The meaning of hajj is "to intend to go to Makkah to perform specific acts at a specific time [of the year]."

---

[1] Recorded by Ahmad and by al-Haakim who declared it authentic. [Also recorded by Abu Dawood. According to al-Albaani, it is sahih. See al-Albaani, Saheeh Sunan Abi Dawood, vol. 1, p. 324.—JZ]

The Umrah [Lesser Visitation]

Umrah (عمرة), linguistically, means "a visit." Legally, it refers to specific actions [performed at specific places] that shall be discussed later.

It is obligatory at least once in one's lifetime.

The Wisdom Behind the Enjoining of Hajj and Umrah

Among the aspects of wisdom behind the Hajj and Umrah is that they purify the soul from the effects of sins so that the person becomes ready for the grace of Allah in the Hereafter. The Prophet (peace be upon him) said,

مَنْ حَجَّ هَذَا الْبَيْتَ فَلَمْ يَرْفُثْ وَلَمْ يَفْسُقْ رَجَعَ كَيَوْمٍ وَلَدَتْهُ أُمُّهُ

"Whoever makes the pilgrimage to this house and does not have sexual intercourse nor does evil shall return [with respect to his sins] like the day on which his mother gave him birth." (Recorded by al-Bukhari.)

Topic One:

The Conditions of the Hajj and Umrah

The Conditions of Obligation

In order for the Hajj to become obligatory, one must meet the following conditions:

(1) Being Muslim.

(2) Being sane.

(3) Being adult.

(4) Being able to make the journey, this includes the presence of the provisions and other righteous travelers to accompany him.

(5) Complete freedom.

(6) In the case of women, another condition is added and that is the existence of an adult male relative within the prohibited degrees of marriage [who can accompany her on the journey]; if she makes pilgrimage without such an escort, she would have committed a sin although her pilgrimage would have been valid.

If a child performs the pilgrimage, it will be considered a valid voluntary pilgrimage but he must still perform the obligatory pilgrimage of Islam after he becomes of age.

If a person who should perform the pilgrimage dies without doing so, wealth is taken from what he has left behind so that someone may perform the pilgrimage on his behalf.

It is not acceptable for a person to perform pilgrimage on another's behalf when he has not done so on his own behalf. It is proper for a capable person to appoint someone to perform a voluntary pilgrimage or umrah on his behalf.

The Different Ways in Which the Pilgrimage Can Be Performed

[The following are the different combinations of performing the hajj or umrah:]

(1) Performing the umrah by itself.

(2) Performing the hajj by itself.

(3) Performing the hajj in connection with the umrah.

(4) Performing the umrah in combination with the hajj but with a break in between.

As for the umrah by itself, it may be performed throughout the days of the year. It is best when the umrah is performed with the hajj or during Ramadhaan.

As for the hajj by itself, this is where the pilgrim intends to perform only the hajj without performing the umrah beforehand or in connection with it.

As for the hajj in connection with the umrah, the acts of the two are combined and it is sufficient to perform one circumambulation and one *sa'ee* (referring to the going back and forth between the mounts of Safa and Marwah).

As for the umrah in combination with the hajj but with a break in between, this is the best way to perform hajj. It is when the person enters the inviolable state for umrah during the months designated for hajj. He makes the *sa'ee*, circumambulation and then comes out of the inviolable state. Then on the eighth day of the month of Dhu-l-Hijjah, he enters the inviolable state for the hajj during that same year. He performs all of the acts of the hajj, including the circumambulation, *sa'ee*, staying at Arafah and so forth. He sacrifices the animal which is obligatory when a person performs this type of hajj or the previous type (the hajj in connection with the umrah).

Topic Three:

The Essential Components of the Hajj and Umrah

There are four essential components for the hajj: entering the inviolable state, circumambulation, *sa'ee* and staying at Arafah. If any of these acts are not performed, the hajj is not valid.

Umrah has three essential components: entering the inviolable state, circumambulation and *sa'ee*. It is not complete except with these acts. The details concerning these essential components are as follows:

The First Essential

The first essential component of the hajj or umrah is entering into the inviolable state. It is the intention to perform one of the types of pilgrimage rites, hajj or umrah, after preparing to enter into that state and removing any sewn clothing.

The Obligatory Aspects of the Inviolable State

The obligatory aspects of the inviolable state are three:

(1) Entering into the state at the proper place: This is the place that is designated by the Lawgiver to enter into the inviolable state, such that it is not allowed to go beyond that point without being in that state for whoever wants to perform hajj or umrah.

(2) Removing all sewn clothing: Men are not allowed to wear gowns, shirts, head caps or scarves and, in fact, the head should not be covered at all. Similarly, they should not wear leather socks unless they cannot find sandals. Women are not to wear face veils or gloves.

(3) The *talbiyyah*: This is the saying of,

$$\text{لَبَّيْكَ اللَّهُمَّ لَبَّيْكَ لَبَّيْكَ لَا شَرِيكَ لَكَ لَبَّيْكَ إِنَّ الْحَمْدَ وَالنِّعْمَةَ}$$

$$\text{لَكَ وَالْمُلْكَ لَا شَرِيكَ لَكَ}$$

"*Labaika-llahumma labaik labaika laa shareeka laka labaik. Inna-l-hamda wa-nimata laka wa-l-mulk. Laa shareeka lak* (O Allah, here I am at your service. You have no partner. Here I am at your service. Verily, all the praise and the grace belong to You, and the Dominion [as well]. You have no partner)."

The pilgrim states these words when he enters into the inviolable state at the appointed location before going beyond that point. It is recommended to repeat these words over and over and, for the men, to say them aloud. One should start saying these words again at every moment of descending, riding, before the beginning of the prayer, after the prayer is finished and so forth. During the umrah, one discontinues saying these words when he starts the circumambulation. During the hajj, one discontinues saying these words upon the throwing of the pebbles at al-Uqbah.

The Second Essential: The Circumambulation

The circumambulation refers to going around the House of Allah seven times. There are seven conditions to this act:

(1) Having the intention at the time of beginning the act.

(2) Being free of any impurities or conditions that nullify a person's state of purity.

(3) Covering the private parts since the circumambulation is like the prayer.

(4) Circumambulating within the confines of the [grand] mosque itself, even if one is far from the House.

(5) Having the House of Allah on one's left side while circumambulating.

(6) Circumambulating the House seven times.

(7) Making each circuit after each other, without any unnecessary breaks.

Recommended Aspects for the Circumambulation

(1) *Al-raml*, this act is recommended for the capable men, but not for women. It refers to the act of jogging during the circuit but with close steps. It is only recommended in the first set of circumambulations when one arrives at the Kaaba, known as *tawaaf al-qudoom*.[1]

(2) Baring the right shoulder,[2] again this is only for the first circumambulation upon arriving in Makkah; it is also for the men only and not the women. It is done during all seven circuits.

(3) Kissing the Black Stone upon beginning the circumambulation and in every circuit thereafter, if possible. It is also recommended to touch the Yemeni corner of the Kaabah.

(4) When beginning the first circuit, one should say, "In the name of Allah and Allah is greatest. O Allah, [I perform this act] with belief in You and attesting to Your book and fulfilling Your pact and following the sunnah of Your prophet."

(5) Making supplications throughout the circumambulation. No specific supplication is required; one may say whatever supplication one is led by Allah to say. However, it is recommended that when ending a circuit to say,

رَبَّنَا آتِنَا فِي الدُّنْيَا حَسَنَةً وَفِي الآخِرَةِ حَسَنَةً وَقِنَا عَذَابَ النَّارِ

"O our Lord, give us in this world good and in the Hereafter good and save us from the punishment of the Fire."

---

[1] Muslim recorded on the authority of ibn Umar that the Prophet made *raml* from the Black Stone on the first three circuits and then walked the last four.

[2] Ahmad recorded that the Prophet (peace be upon him) and his Companions made the Umrah from al-Jaraanah and uncovered their right shoulders, putting their garments under their right arm pits and throwing them over the left shoulder.

(6) Making supplications at al-Multazim after finishing the circumambulation. Al-Multazim is the place between the door to the Kaabah and the Black Stone.

(7) After finishing the circuits, one should pray two *rakat*s behind the "station of Abraham," reciting *soorahs al-Kafiroon* and *al-Ikhlaas* after *al-Faatihah*.

(8) Drink some water from the well of Zamzam and, in fact, one should drink one's fill of it after finishing the two *rakat*s.

(9) One should return to the Black Stone and touch it before moving on to the *sa'ee*.

The Third Essential: The *Sa'ee*

The *sa'ee* is the walking back and forth between the mounts of al-Safa and al-Marwah with the intention of worship. It is an essential component of both the hajj and the umrah.

The Conditions of the *Sa'ee*

(1) The intention, for the Prophet (peace be upon him) said,

$$ إِنَّمَا الأَعْمَالُ بِالنِّيَّاتِ $$

"Surely, all actions are but driven by intentions." (Recorded by al-Bukhari.)

(2) It must be in the proper chronological order with respect to the circumambulation; that is, the circumambulation must be done first followed by the *sa'ee*.

(3) Each of its circuits must be done right after the other; however, a small break does not cause any harm, especially if there is some need for it.

(4) One must complete seven trips [four going and three returning, not a total of seven going and coming]. If one trip or part of one trip is missing, it will not be sufficient. Its correctness depends on all of the trips being completed.

(5) It must be performed after a correct and valid circumambulation, regardless of whether that circumambulation be of an obligatory or recommended nature.

The Recommended Acts of the *Sa'ee*

(1) Jogging between the two green markers; these mark the places between which Haajr, the mother of Ismaeel, paced back and forth. This is recommended for men who have the ability to do so and not for those who are weak or for women.

(2) One should stop at or on top of al-Safa and al-Marwah to supplicate.

(3) One should make supplications during each of the trips between al-Safa and al-Marwah.

(4) One should say, "*Allaahu akbar* (Allah is greatest)" three times upon ascending both al-Safa and al-Marwah each time one reaches them; one should also say,

لا إِلَهَ إِلاَّ اللَّهُ وَحْدَهُ لا شَرِيكَ لَهُ لَهُ الْمُلْكُ وَلَهُ الْحَمْدُ وَهُوَ
عَلَى كُلِّ شَيْءٍ قَدِيرٌ صَدَقَ وَعْدَهُ وَنَصَرَ عَبْدَهُ وَهَزَمَ الأَحْزَابَ
وَحْدَهُ

"There is none worthy of worship except Allah, the One, for whom there is no partner. To Him belongs the dominion and to Him is the praise. And He has power over all things. He fulfilled His promise, supported His servant and vanquished the parties by Himself."

(5) The *sa'ee* should be performed immediately after the circumambulation such that there is no break between them without a valid reason.

The Fourth Essential: Stopping at Arafah

The fourth essential act is stopping at Arafah. What this actually means is being present at the place known as Arafah, for a small portion of time or more, with the intention of stopping there between the time of noon on the tenth of Dhu-l-Hijjah until dawn on the tenth of Dhu-l-Hijjah. If a person misses this stopping at Arafah, he has missed the entire hajj and should then simply perform umrah and make up that hajj at a later time. He must also make a sacrifice, even if he had not made that a part of his rites prior. If an enemy is preventing one from reaching the House of Allah, he should make a sacrifice and then leave the inviolable state. If he is prevented due to an illness or running out of expenditures and he had laid down the condition, "I become free of the inviolable state wherever I am confined," he leaves the inviolable state and there is no other act he must perform. However, if he did not make that condition, he must make a sacrifice that is easy upon him.

Topic Three:
The Obligatory Acts of the Hajj and Umrah

The Obligatory Acts of the Hajj

The obligatory acts of the hajj are seven:
(1) Entering the inviolable state before preceding beyond the required locations.

(2) Staying at Arafah until sunset for the one who is there during the daytime.

(3) Spending the night— at least until after midnight— before the Day of Sacrifice at Muzdalifah.

(4) Residing in Mina during the days of *Tashreeq*.

(5) Throwing the pebbles in their proper order.

(6) Shaving or cutting one's hair.

(7) Performing the farewell circumambulation.

The Obligatory Acts of the Umrah

The obligatory acts of the umrah are two:

(1) Entering into the inviolable state— for those who live in Makkah it is from wherever they are and for those from outside it is at the appointed locations.

(2) Shaving or cutting the hair.

Important Notes

If a person fails to perform one of the essential acts, his rites are not complete unless he performs it.

If a person fails to perform an obligatory act, this must be compensated for by sacrificing an animal.

If a person fails to perform a recommended act, there is nothing he must then do.

Topic Four:

Acts Forbidden for One in the Inviolable State

The forbidden acts are deeds that if the person making hajj or umrah does any of them, it is obligatory upon him to make a sacrifice, fast or feed others. The following are forbidden for the male or the female in the inviolable state:

(1) Cutting one's hair on any part of the body.

(2) Trimming the finger or toe nails.

(3) Covering the head [for men] and covering the face for women, unless men who are not related to them should be passing by.

(4) Wearing sewn clothing by men, such as a long shirt or pants.

(5) Using perfume.

(6) Killing land game that is [normally] permissible to eat.

(7) Getting married.

(8) Having sexual intercourse; if this were done before the "first lessening of the restrictions,"[1] all the rites then become void. They must then sacrifice a camel and continue in their hajj and make up the hajj in the following year. If that were done after the "first lessening of the restrictions," then the rites do not become void but they must sacrifice a sheep.

(9) Having contact with women in a manner less than sexual intercourse; if the man ejaculates, he must sacrifice a camel. If he does not, then he must sacrifice a sheep. In either case, though, the rites of his hajj have not been voided.

The ruling for women is the same as for men concerning these issues except that she is allowed to wear sewn clothing. She may wear whatever she wills as long as it is not a display of beauty. She covers her head but uncovers her face, not covering it unless there are men who are not related to her present.

The "first lessening of the restrictions" occurs after a person has performed any two of the following three acts: (1) the circumambulation, (2) the throwing of the pebbles or (3) the shaving or cutting of the hair.

If a woman gets her menses while she was intending to perform the hajj followed by the umrah with a break in between and she fears that she will miss the hajj, she enters

---

[1] This is defined below.

into the inviolable state with her menses and she makes her rites as the hajj combined with the umrah. The menstruating woman and the woman with post-partum bleeding perform all of the rites of the hajj save for the circumambulation of the House of Allah.

It is allowed for the pilgrim to slaughter livestock and similar animals. Furthermore, he may kill any harmful animals, such as lions, wolves, tigers, cheetahs, snakes, scorpions, rats and any harmful animal. He may also kill water animals and eat them.

It is forbidden for a pilgrim or a non-pilgrim to cut the shrubbery of the inviolable sanctuary or to cut its grasses, except for *idhkhar* which is type of grass that may be cut. It is forbidden for him to kill game animals. If he does so, he must fulfill the penalty or "ransom". It is also forbidden to hunt the game of Madinah or to cut its shrubbery, although there is no penalty or ransom in that case.

If someone has a valid excuse and is forced to do one of the above mentioned forbidden acts, except for sexual intercourse, such as shaving one's hair or wearing sewn clothing, he may do so but he has to fulfill the penalty. He has a choice between (a) fasting three days, (b) feeding sixty poor people, each one with a *mudd* (what two hands cupped together can hold) of wheat, rice or so on or (c) slaughtering a sheep.

If a person does any of the above mentioned forbidden acts due to ignorance, forgetfulness or coercion, then there is no sin upon him and no penalty. This is based on Allah's statement,

$$رَبَّنَا لَا تُؤَاخِذْنَا إِنْ نَسِينَا أَوْ أَخْطَأْنَا$$

"Our Lord! Do not take us to task if we forget or fall into error" (*al-Baqarah* 286). [This is a supplication that is confirmed in a hadith that Allah has responded to positively.]

If a pilgrim kills a land game and there is a comparable animal that he can sacrifice, he has the choice between getting such an animal, sacrificing it and distributing its meat among the poor who live in the area of the Grand Mosque, or taking the value of the animal and buying food to feed the poor, with each of them receiving a *mudd*[1] worth of food, or fasting one day for every *mudd* of food that he would have given. If there is no comparable animal to the one killed, he has a choice between buying its value's worth of food and distributing it among the poor who live in the area or fasting one day for each *mudd* of food that he would have given.

The ransom or penalty for engaging in contact with women without ejaculation is the same as the penalty for the one who has a valid excuse to violate one of the acts: he either fasts, feeds the poor or slaughters a sheep.

If a person has sexual intercourse during the hajj and before the "first lessening of the restrictions," he must sacrifice a camel. If he is not able to, he must fast three days during the hajj and then another seven upon his return to his land. If the act was after the "first lessening of the restrictions," then his ransom is the same as the one who has a valid excuse to violate one of the acts of hajj, as described above.

The one who performs the hajj with the umrah, in either fashion, and who is not from the Makkah area, must sacrifice a sheep [as part of the rites of hajj]. Another option is for seven people to join together in the sacrifice of a camel or cattle. If one is not able to perform the sacrifice, he must fast three days during the hajj and then another seven days when he returns to his home.

The one who is prevented from reaching Makkah and performing his hajj must make a sacrifice. If he is not able to, he must fast ten days before he leaves the inviolable state.

---

[1] A *mudd* is what a man with normal sized hands can hold with his two hands held together in the shape of a bowl.

If someone violates the restrictions more than once but with acts all of the same violation and he had not yet performed the ransom, then he performs the ransom only once— with the exception of killing more than one game animal. However, if he violates the restrictions more than once by doing different violating acts, such as cutting his hair and then clipping his nails, he must then perform the ransom for every separate type of violation he did.

Topic Five:

The Specific Times and Locations for Entering into the Inviolable State

There are specific times and specific locations for entering into the inviolable state.

The specific time for entering into the inviolable state is during the "months of Hajj," which are Shawaal, Dhu-l-Qaaidah and Dhu-l-Hijjah.

The specific locations for the people who want to make hajj or umrah are five. They are:

(1) Dhu-l-Halaifah: This is the appointed place for the people of Madinah and those who pass through it. It is 435 kilometers from Makkah. It is the appointed place that is the furthest from Makkah.

(2) Al-Juhfah: This is the appointed place for the people of al-Shaam (Syria, Palestine, Jordan, Lebanon region) and Egypt and those who are from the same direction or pass through those areas. It is a village close to Raabigh. It is 180 kilometers from Makkah. Today, people enter the inviolable state at Raabigh.

(3) Yalamlam: This is the appointed location for the people of Yemen and surrounding areas and those who pass

through that area. Yalamlam is a valley about 92 kilometers from Makkah.

(4) Qarn al-Manaazil is the appointed location for those coming from or through Najd or Taaif. Today, it is known as *al-Seel al-Kabeer*. It is 75 kilometers from Makkah. The place to enter into the inviolable state is at the top of Qarn al-Manaazil.

(5) Dhaat Irq: This is the appointed location for those from or going through Iraq, Khurasan, central and north Najd and the surrounding areas. It is a valley and is also called al-Dhareebah. It is about 100 kilometers from Makkah.

Those are the appointed places for the people of those areas or others who transverse through those lands wanting to make hajj or umrah.

Whoever is living already within the appointed places enters the inviolable state wherever he wills, to the point that the people of Makkah enter the state within Makkah itself. If a Makkan wants to make hajj, he enters the inviolable state within Makkah. If he wants to make umrah, he goes outside of the limits of the sacred mosque and enters the inviolable state there.

If a person does not exactly pass through one of the appointed locations, he enters the inviolable state at a location parallel to the closest appointed spot. He enters the inviolable state as he passes that location whether it be by plane, car, bus or whatever.

It is not allowed for a person making hajj or umrah to pass beyond the appointed locations without entering into the inviolable state. If a person passes through them without entering into the inviolable state, he must go back to them and enter into the inviolable state from there. If he does not go back and he enters into the inviolable state from wherever he is, he must sacrifice an animal and his hajj or umrah will be valid. If he enters the inviolable state before reaching the appointed locations, his act is valid but reprehensible.

Topic Six:

The Sacrifice and *Aqeeqah*

The Sacrifice

This is the camel, cattle or sheep/goat that is sacrificed on the Day of Sacrifice or days of Tashreeq (11th through 13th of Dhu-l-Hijjah) with the intention of a sacrifice. This is a sunnah or recommended act.

The Timing of the Sacrifice

The sacrifice is to be done from after the Eid Prayer on the Day of Sacrifice until the end of the days of *Tashreeq* (the 13th of Dhu-l-Hijjah).

It is recommended to divide the slaughtered animal into three portions: the person eats one-third, gives one third away as a gift and gives the last third away as charity. There is great merit to the sacrifice as the wealth is spread around and the poor are benefited and their needs are met.

An animal does not suffice as a sacrificial animal or the animal of the hajj unless it be a female camel of at least five years old, a cow of at least two years old, a fat sheep of at least six months or a goat of at least one year.

It is sufficient for one person to slaughter a sheep or for seven to join together in a camel or cow. It is permissible for a sheep, camel or cow to be slaughtered on behalf of oneself or the members of one's family. The slaughtered animal must be free of any types of defects.

It is recommended to slaughter on behalf of the living and permissible to do so on behalf of someone who has died. For the one who [although is not performing the hajj but] is going to perform the sacrifice, it is not permissible for him to remove any of his hair or skin during the first ten days of the month of Dhu-l-Hijjah. It is recommended for him to fast those days and to increase his good deeds therein.

The *Aqeeqah*

The *aqeeqah* is the animal that is slaughtered at the time a child is born. It is a recommended act. For a boy, two sheep should be slaughtered; for a girl, only one sheep is slaughtered. This slaughtering is to take place on the seventh day and the child is also named on that day, has his hair cut and the weight of his hair in silver is given in charity. If that day is missed, it is to be done on the fourteenth day. If that day is also missed, it is done on the twenty-first day. After that, it is done at any time. It is recommended not to break the bones of the animal. The *aqeeqah* is a way of expressing thanks to Allah for the continuous blessings one receives as well as the child just received.

Dr. Saalih al-Sadlaan

Chapter Six:
Jihad

Definition

Jihad (حــــهاد) is to expend every effort and ability in fighting against the disbelievers.

The Wisdom Behind Its Legislation

Jihad is the apex of Islam and the most virtuous of the voluntary deeds. Allah has legislated it to meet the following goals:

(1) To make the word of Allah supreme and all religion only for Allah.

(2) For the happiness of mankind and to release them from darkness into light.

(3) To establish justice on the earth, by establishing the truth and eradicating falsehood and preventing oppression and evil.

(4) To spread the religion, protect the Muslims and foil the stratagem of the enemies.

The Legal Status of the Jihad

Jihad is a communal obligation. If enough members of the community fulfill this responsibility, the rest of the members are absolved of any responsibility. However, under the following circumstances it becomes obligatory upon everyone who has the ability to perform it:

(1) If the person is in the rows of those actually engaged in fighting.

(2) If the enemy has appeared in the people's land.

(3) If the Imam calls for all to go out to the jihad.

The Conditions for Jihad to Be Obligatory

[In general, jihad is only obligatory upon a person when he meets the following conditions:]

(1) Being a Muslim.

(2) Being sane.

(3) Being adult.

(4) Being male.

(5) Being free of physical defects (such as illness, blindness, being lame).

(6) Having the needed expenditures.

The Different Types of Jihad

Jihad can be divided into the following four types:

(1) Jihad against the soul: This refers to striving against one's soul to make it learn about the religion, act upon those teachings, call others to it and bear with patience the harm that comes as a result of calling others to the straight path.

(2) Jihad against Satan: This is struggling against Satan with respect to the doubts and desires that he casts into the heart of man.

(3) Jihad against the disbelievers and hypocrites: This is done with the heart, tongue, wealth and hand.

(4) Jihad against the wrongdoers, heretics and evil folk: This is best to be done with one's hand. If one is not able

to do that, then with one's tongue. If one is not able to do that either, then with one's heart.

The Virtues with Allah Awaiting the Martyr

There are seven benefits with Allah awaiting the martyr: he will be forgiven from the moment of his first drop of blood, he shall see his abode in Paradise, he shall be rescued from the punishment of the grave, he will be saved from the great frightening, he shall wear the crown of faith, he shall get married from the *haur al-ain* [spouses in Paradise] and he shall intercede for seventy of his relatives.

Etiquette of War

The etiquette of war in Islam includes the following points: those fighting cannot betray their trusts, women and children are not to be killed if they are not combatants, the fighters are to be free of arrogance and deceit, they should not wish to have to face the enemy, they should supplicate for victory and assistance from Allah, such as by saying, "O Allah, revealer of the book, mover of the clouds, dispenser of the clans, vanquish them and support us against them."

It is forbidden to flee from the fighting except under two circumstances: (1) as a way of fending off the fighting or (2) as a way of joining back with the troops.

The Captives of War

The captives of war are divided into two categories:
(1) Women and children who are made slaves.
(2) Fighting men for whom the leader has three choices: set them free, ransom them or kill them.

The leader must review the troops as they set out. He must keep them from deserting or causing dissent. The leader should not seek any assistance from disbelievers except in cases of dire necessity. He should prepare the provisions and travel with the army in a kind manner. He should seek the best place for them to camp and he should prevent the army from committing any evil or sins. He should speak to them in a way that will strengthen their conviction and make them seek martyrdom. He should order them to be patient. He should divide up the army and appoint specialists and guards over them. He should also send spies out to check on the enemy. He should expel any spies for the enemy from the troops. He should consult the religious and intelligent people concerning the matters of jihad.

How the Army Should Treat Their Leader

The army should obey their leader and be patient with him. It is not allowed for them to fight except by his permission, unless they have been hit by a surprise attack and they fear the spread of harm. If the enemy requests a truce or if the fighting is during the sacred months, the Muslims should then sign a truce.

Part Two: Transactions among Humans

This part shall be comprised of the following chapters:
Chapter One: Business Transactions
Chapter Two: Interest
Chapter Three: Lease and Rentals
Chapter Four: Religious Endowments
Chapter Five: Bequests

Dr. Saalih al-Sadlaan

Chapter One:
Business Transactions

This chapter is comprised of an introduction and the following two topics:

Topic 1: The essential components and conditions of a business transaction;

Topic 2: Prohibited sales transactions.

Introduction

Lexical and Legal Definition of *Bai'*

Bai' (بيع) is the verbal noun of *baa'*. It is the exchange of wealth for wealth or the giving of one item in exchange for something else in its place.

From a legal point of view, buying and selling refers to a contract involving an exchange of wealth which results in the permanent ownership of an item or a usufruct and which is not done for the sake of getting closer to Allah.

Legal buying and selling is permissible, as the Book, sunnah, consensus and reasoning all indicate its permissibility.

The Wisdom Behind Legalizing Buying and Selling

Since money, merchandise and goods are distributed among people in general and there is a need for humans to have what is in the hands of their associates who will not sacrifice it without something in exchange, there is a strong need for the permissibility of buying, selling and meeting one's goals. For these reasons, Allah has permitted buying and selling to fulfill those benefits and needs.

Topic One:

The Essential Components and Conditions for Buying and Selling

The Essential Components of Buying and Selling

The essential components of a business transaction are:

(1) The form it takes, consisting of an offer and acceptance.

(2) The two who take part in the transaction, the buyer and the seller.

(3) The object of the contract: the price and what the price is being used to purchase.

The Form of the Transaction

The form of the transaction refers to the offer and acceptance. It is an indication of approval and gladness with the transaction. The seller might say, "I sell this or give this to you or put this in your possession for such and such a price." The buyer may say, "I then buy this or possess this or purchase this or accept this," and so on. A transaction is also valid by a [clear, well-known] action by one of the two parties or by both parties.

Transactions Over the Phone

If people speak over the phone, this is considered a contractual meeting. It ends with the end of the phone conversation. This is because customary practices are defining rules concerning the beginning or ending of a contractual meeting.

The Conditions for a Sound Business Transaction

In order for a business transaction to be sound and valid, the following seven conditions must be met:

(1) Both the buyer and the seller, or their representatives, must approve of the transaction.

(2) It must be the case that both of them are allowed to enter into a transaction, such that they are both free, legally capable and competent.

(3) The merchandise that is being sold must be something whose usufruct is permissible. It is not allowed to sell something that has no [legal] benefit to them and it is not allowed to sell something whose benefit is forbidden, such as alcohol or pork. Similarly, it is not allowed to sell something that is only permissible in cases of necessity, such as carrion.

(4) The seller must own what he is selling or have permission to sell it at the time of the contract.

(5) The item sold must be known by its description or by being seen.

(6) The price must be known.

(7) The thing being sold must be something that the seller is able to hand over to the buyer; it is not allowed to sell the street or birds flying the sky and so forth.

Stipulations in the Contract

Stipulations in the contract are of two types: sound and binding or illegal and voiding of the contract.

Sound stipulations include the stipulation to delay all or part of the payment or a stipulation for collateral or specific guarantee. That is for the benefit of the contract itself. Another example is the condition of a specific quality in the transaction. The Prophet (peace be upon him) said,

$$\text{الْمُسْلِمُونَ عَلَى شُرُوطِهِمْ}$$

"The Muslims abide by their stipulations." Recorded by Ahmad and Abu Dawood.[1] It is also acceptable for the seller to stipulate upon the buyer that he will use the usufruct of what he is selling for a specified period of time, such as remaining to live in a house for one month.

The invalid conditions include: conditions that are invalid and void the contract, such as a condition involving two contracts in one, for example, an advanced payment combined with a loan, a sale with a lease and so forth. Some non-valid conditions do not void the contract, only the condition itself is considered not valid, such as the condition that guarantees that an investment will not lose money or something in which someone, in reality, neither sells the item nor gives it away. These conditions are not valid unless they are done for a particular benefit [consistent with the overall purpose of a contract], in which case they are sound.

---

[1] According to al-Albaani, this hadith is *sahih*. See al-Albaani, *Saheeh al-Jaami*, vol. 2, p. 1138.—JZ

Topic Two:
Prohibited Transactions

Islam permits every sale that produces good and blessings. It forbids every transaction that contains aspects of ignorance, great risk or harm to the people in the marketplace or causes harsh feelings in the heart. Such dealings bring about hatred, disputes and fighting. These prohibited types of transactions include the following:

(1) *al-Mulaamasah*: This is when the seller tells the buyer, for example, "Any garment you touched is yours for such and such." This type of sale is not valid because it involves ignorance [concerning which garment is going to be bought] and risk.

(2) *al-Munaabidhah*: This is where the seller tells the buyer, "Any garment you fling to me is yours for such and such price." Again, this type of sale is not valid because of the existence of ignorance and risk.

(3) *Bai al-Hasaah*: This is where one says, for example, "Throw this pebble and whatever merchandise it lands on is yours for such and such price." Again, this type of sale is not valid due to the ignorance and risk involved.

(4) *Bai al-Najash*: This is where a person bids up the price on something without having the intention to buy it. This type of sale is forbidden because it is a type of deception and tricking of the buyer.

(5) Having two sales in one sale: This is, for example, when one person says to another, "I sell you this on the condition that you sell that to me," or, "on the condition that you also buy that from me." Another example is where the person says, "I will sell this to you for ten dollars right now or twenty over time," and then they part from one another without stating which one they agree to. This kind of sale is not valid. This is because the second sale is conditional on the

first and because the price of the second has not been established.

(6) A city-dweller selling to a bedouin [outside of the city]: This is the sale wherein the seller sells the item for a price greater than its daily price [in the city while the bedouin is unaware of that fact].

(7) A brother selling against his brother in Islam: For example, he says to someone who is about to buy something for ten dollars from someone else, "I can sell the same to you for nine."

(8) Selling merchandise before one actually takes possession of it.

(9) *Bai al-Eenah*: This is where a person buys something from somebody else on credit and then sells it back to him for a lower cash price.

(10) Buying or selling after the second call to prayer for the Friday Prayer for the one who is obliged to attend the Friday Prayer.

Chapter Two:
Riba (Interest) and Its Rulings

This chapter is composed of an introduction and the following three topics:

Topic 1: The different types of *riba* (interest);

Topic 2: The doors that Islam opens that frees one from *riba*;

Topic 3: Interest paid out by banks and its status.

Introduction

The Definition of *Riba*

Lexically, *riba* (ربا) means an addition or an increase. One says, *"rabaa al-maal,"* if the wealth increased or grew. It is used in a general sense to refer to any transaction which is forbidden.

In the terminology of the jurists, *riba* refers to an increase in particular things or a contract to exchange something particular but not for its known equivalent according to the criteria of the law at the time of the contract or with a delay in the exchange of both or either of them.

The Wisdom Behind the Prohibition of *Riba*

Islam forbids *riba* due to the following reasons:

(1) There is no relation between the effort put out and the return as the one who lends money on interest does not

expend any effort or work nor does he bear any risk, with respect to what he will earn and what he will own of gain.

(2) The society's economy will be depressed due to the lender's loitering and not working. They will be content with resting and laziness as they look forward to their profits from their interest and the hardships that they put on the debtors due to the interest requirements.

(3) The morale of the society will also collapse as there is no cooperation between its members; this will definitely lead to the breaking up of society and the spreading of rapaciousness and selfishness instead of sacrifice, love and giving to others.

(4) The society will be divided into disputing classes, a class of exploiters and rulers over capital and a class of poor and oppressed whose efforts and weariness will be exploited without due right.

Topic One:

The Types of *Riba*

According to most scholars, *riba* is of two types:

(1) *Riba al-naseeah*: *Al-naseeah* means delay and deferment. *Riba al-naseeah* is an increased amount in one of the exchanged items for a delay in the payment for the item.

(2) *Riba al-fadhl*: Lexically, *al-fadhl* means the opposite of decrease or shortage. So *riba al-fadhl* is an addition in the amount of one of the two exchanged items which are of the same genus or class— of those items for which *riba al-fadhl* applies, such as gold in exchange for more gold or wheat in exchange for more wheat. This is also known as *riba al-bai'* (*riba* of buying and selling) and *al-riba al-khafi* (the hidden *riba*).

The Shafi'ees add a third category known as *riba al-yad* wherein taking possession of one or both of the exchanged items is deferred. Others add a fourth type known as *riba al-qardh* wherein a loan is given but it is stipulated that the creditor will receive some other benefit [more than simply receiving his money back].

In reality, those two categories do not fall outside of the realm of the two categories stated above.

Contemporary economists divide interest into [that accruing from] consumption loans and [that accruing from] production loans.

(1) Interest on consumption loans is that additional money paid back on a loan that is used to purchase consumption needs such as food, drink, medicine and so forth.

(2) Interest on production loans is that paid back on loans used for investment purposes such as manufacturing, farming or specific business purposes.

They also divide interest into two other categories:

(1) Compound interest: This is what makes the percentage of interest large.

(2) Simple interest: This is wherein the interest rate is low.[1]

Islam's prohibition of interest includes any kind of dealing with it, regardless of whether it is *riba fadhl* or *riba naseeah* or if the interest amount is large or small or if it is interest on a consumption loan or a production loan. All of those varieties fall under the wording of prohibition in Allah's statement,

وَأَحَلَّ اللَّهُ الْبَيْعَ وَحَرَّمَ الرِّبَا

"Allah has permitted trade and forbidden *riba*" (*al-Baqarah* 275).

---

[1] This is not actual the difference between compound and simple interest but such is what is stated in the text.—JZ

Topic Two:
The Doors That Islam Opens to Freedom from
Riba

Islam has opened many ways to bring about the end of *riba* and make people not in need of resorting to it. These include the following types of dealings:

(1) Islam allows *mudhaarabah* companies. These are companies in which the capital is provided by one person while another person provides the labor. The profit from the venture is divided between the two of them according to the division they have agreed upon. If any losses occur, they fall solely on the capital provider. The one who provided his work and effort does not face any other loss other than losing his time and effort.

(2) Islam allows *salam* purchases. This is where one pays for something now but its delivery is in the future. If a person is in need of cash, he may sell the product of his work at a reasonable price for future delivery. However, the stipulations that are discussed in the books of fiqh must be met for this type of transaction to be valid.

(3) Islam allows purchases with deferred payments wherein the price of the good is increased over what it would be if the item were paid for with cash. Islam has permitted this to make it easier for people to meet their needs and in order to give them a way of escaping from interest.

(4) Islam encourages the establishing of institutions that will give loans, interest-free and for the sake of Allah, regardless of whether these loans be at the level of individuals, organizations or the government. This is in fulfillment of the principle of social security and support among the Muslim nation.

(5) Islam has also legislated the giving of zakaat to those debtors in need, to the poor who do not have possessions,

to the stranger who is cut off from his wealth and so forth. This is all meant to satisfy their needs, improve their condition and raise their position.

These are some of the most important means Islam opens to all individuals of society to fulfill their needs and to preserve their nobility as humans. By such means, also, they may attain their noble goals of fulfilling their needs and allowing their deeds and investments to prosper.

Topic Three:
Interest Paid by Banks

Al-fawaaid [the Arabic term used for the interest paid by modern-day banks] is the plural of "benefit". It is used by economists to refer to the additional money that is paid by the bank to those who have savings accounts or what the bank receives when they lend money. It is a type of *riba*. Indeed, it is the essence of *riba* in itself, even though they may use a different name for it. There is no doubt that it is from the *riba* that is forbidden in the Quran, sunnah and consensus.

It has been narrated that there is a consensus that it is forbidden to stipulate any increase payments for a loan. In fact, what they are offering is not really a loan [from the Islamic perspective]. As the *mufti* of the land of Saudi Arabia, Shaikh Muhammad ibn Ibraaheem said, "In reality, what they call a loan is not a loan. This is because what is meant by 'loan' [from the Islamic perspective] is a goodly loan and assisting loan. Although on the surface these loans look like that, in reality they are a sale of dollars for other dollars on credit with the profit known and stipulated. By this it is known that the interest that is taken by the banks on the loans they give out and which they give to holders of savings accounts is completely equivalent to interest. Both of them are of the meaning of 'an increase.' It is proper to call one the same as the other."

Chapter Three: Leasing, Renting and Hiring

This chapter is composed of an introduction and the following two topics:

Topic 1: The conditions for leasing and hiring;

Topic 2: Issues related to leasing and renting.

Introduction

Definition of *Ijaarah* (Leasing, Renting or Hiring)

Ijaarah (إجارة) refers to a contract for the usufruct of a permissible, known thing for a specified time period.

Its Legal Status

It is permissible and is a contract binding upon both parties.

The Wisdom Behind Its Sanctioning

Ijaarah is a way of exchanging benefits between humans. Humans are in need of tools for work, houses in which to live, animals, cars, modes of transportation and so on. Permitting *ijaarah* makes things easier for people and allows them to meet their needs.

Two Types of *Ijaarah*

There are two types of *ijaarah*:

(1) Renting a specific item, such as, "I rent this house or car to you."

(2) Hiring someone for work, as in hiring someone to build a house or work the land and so forth.

Topic One:

Conditions Required for Leasing and What is Being Hired or Leased

The Conditions for Leasing

The conditions for leasing [or hiring] are four:

(1) It must be let out by one who has the right to deal in the item being leased or rented.

(2) The usufruct or service must be specifically identified, such as living in a house, serving a person or teaching some knowledge.

(3) The payment must be specified.

(4) The usufruct or service must be something permissible, such as a house to live in. Such a contract is not valid if it is for something forbidden, such as for prostitution, singing, making a building into a church, selling alcohol and so on.

Riding in a car, plane or ship or giving one's clothing to a tailor for shortening or sewing or renting some mode of transport without first making a contract is considered permissible because it is something known and done customarily [therefore, the details of it are understood and need not be stated]. The customary practices in those and other similar matters take the place of some specific statement [or agreement].

Conditions for What is Being Leased or Hired

The conditions for the article or service being hired are that it must be known, either by sight or description, the contract is for its use and not its parts, the lessee has the ability to hand over the item, it meets the need for which it is intended, and the lessee either owns it or has permission to lease it.

Topic Two:

Issues Related to *Ijaarah*

It is acceptable to lease an endowment. If the lessee dies, the endowment passes on to those after him and the contract is not dissolved. The lessee shall have his portion of the wages.

Anything that is forbidden to sell is also forbidden to lease out or hire except for an endowment, a free person and a slave who has given birth to a child for her master.

The lease contract is nullified if the article being leased is destroyed and its use comes to an end.

It is permissible to receive wages for teaching, building mosques and so forth. However, receiving wages for performing hajj [on another's behalf] is allowed only in the case of need.

If the Imam, caller to prayer or teacher of the Quran receives a stipend from the public treasury or receives remuneration without conditions, such is permissible for them.

The lessor does not have to pay for the loss of an item if it is destroyed while in his possession as long as he was not negligent or did not himself cause any harm to the item.

The right to payment becomes obligatory when the contract is signed; one must make the payment when the item leased is handed over. However, it is permissible if the two parties agree on a delayed payment or payment over time. The worker deserves his wages as soon as he finishes his work.

Chapter Four:
Endowments

This chapter has an introduction and a discussion of the following three topics:

Topic 1: The types of endowments;

Topic 2: Conditions of an endowment;

Topic 3: The difference between an endowment and a bequest.

Introduction

Lexical and Legal Definition of an Endowment

Lexically, *waqf* (وقف) is a verbal noun whose plural is *auqaaf*. One says, *"waqafa shai"* if something is retained or withheld. In legal terms, it refers to retaining a property or source while distributing its proceeds or returns.

The Basis for the Legality of Endowments

The basis for the legality of endowments is in the confirmed sunnah of the Messenger of Allah (peace be upon him) as well as in the consensus of the Muslim nation.

As for the sunnah, al-Bukhari and Muslim record that Umar said to the Messenger of Allah (peace be upon him), "O Messenger of Allah, I received wealth in Khaibar and I have never received any wealth more dear to me. What do you order me to do with it?" The Messenger of Allah (peace be upon him) replied,

إن شئت حبست أصلها وتصدقت بها

"If you wish, you may retain the property while giving [its proceeds] away in charity." Umar did so on the condition that its property would not be sold, given as a gift or inherited. [Recorded by al-Bukhari.] Umar gave the proceeds in charity to the poor, his relatives, slaves buying their freedom, warriors fighting for the sake of Allah, travelers and visitors. There is no sin upon the person who is in charge of the endowment if he eats from it according to what is customary or if he feeds a friend an amount which is not great.

Endowments are something that are particular to the Muslims. Jaabir said, "None of the Companions of the Prophet (peace be upon him) would ever be of means except that he would establish an endowment." This shows that what most people do today is the opposite of what was known during the time of the Companions. Today, people only know bequests and they are ignorant about endowments.

The Wisdom Behind Sanctioning Endowments

(1) Those to whom Allah has been most generous by bestowing upon them riches and ease are hereby encouraged to increase their acts of obedience and acts getting them closer to Allah by specifying a certain portion of their wealth [to be used as a charitable endowment]. [This property will then] stay and the proceeds will continue to be produced [and given away], so that one does not have to fear that after his death the wealth may pass on to one who will not preserve it or keep it properly, making his efforts go to ruin and his descendents needy and in hardship. In order to prevent all of those possibilities and in order for the person himself to participate

in the good deeds, the concept of the endowment has been sanctioned in the lifetime of the person so that he may himself be part of it and put it where he wants so that its proceeds will continue to be beneficial after his lifetime as they were during his life.

(2) Endowments are a main cause of the establishment and maintenance of mosques, schools, hospices and similar other good deeds. Most of the mosques throughout history were established as endowments. In fact, all of the items that a mosque needs—of carpets, cleaning and sustenance for those maintain it—were and still are supported by the endowments.

The Wording of the Endowment

Some words for stating an endowment are explicit, such as, "I endow this," "I keep this for such and such purpose." Others are less explicit and more figurative, such as, "I give this in charity," "I give this forever," and so forth.

The figurative terms indicate an endowment in one of three ways:

(1) The intention, if spoken and intended by one of those figurative terms, becomes an endowment.

(2) If the figurative terms are used in conjunction with other explicit or figurative terms [making the matter clear], such as, "I give this in charity as an endowment," or, "permanently," and so on, [there is an endowment].

(3) A description of something as having the characteristics of an endowment, such as saying, "This is forbidden [for anyone to dispense with], it cannot be sold or given as a gift," [indicates an endowment].

In the same way that endowments may be made by one's clear or figurative speech, they may also be made by one's actions, as in the case where a person sets up a mosque on his land and announces to the people to come and pray in it.

Topic One:

The Types of Endowments and What May Be Given as Endowments

Types of Endowments

With respect to who receives the first benefits of the endowments, endowments may be divided into two types: charitable and familial.

(1) Charitable endowments: This is where the first benefits of an endowment go to a charitable cause, even if only for a limited time period. After that time period, the benefits may be to a specific person or specific people. An example of this nature would be someone giving his land for a hospital or school and then after some time the land reverts to his children.

(2) Familial endowments: This is where the person, at the outset, may designate the proceeds to go to himself or another specific person or people and then, at the end, to charitable causes. For example, he may make an endowment for himself and then for his children and, after them, for general charitable causes.

What is Proper to Be Made Endowments

There is a consensus that existing wealth that has a value to it [from the Islamic perspective], made up of immovable property, such as land or buildings, may be given as endowments. Movable property such as books, clothing, animals and weaponry may also be given. The Messenger of Allah (peace be upon him) said,

$$\text{وَأَمَّا خَالِدٌ فَإِنَّكُمْ تَظْلِمُونَ خَالِدًا قَدِ احْتَبَسَ أَدْرَاعَهُ وَأَعْتُدَهُ}$$

$$\text{فِي سَبِيلِ اللَّهِ}$$

As for Khaalid, you have done him wrong [by asking him for zakaat] as he is keeping his armor [as an endowment] and having it prepared for [fighting for] the sake of Allah." [Recorded by al-Bukhari.] The agreement of the nation is that one may also give as an endowment the rugs, mats and lamps in the mosques; there is no objection to those types of endowments.

Jewelry may also be made an endowment for wearing and lending. This is because it is an article that may be benefited from perpetually and hence one may give it as an endowment like immovable property.

Topic Two:

The Conditions for an Endowment

The endowment is built upon two important factors: the one giving the endowment and the thing that is given as an endowment. Each one has specific conditions that it must meet.

Conditions for the One Making the Endowment

There are certain conditions that the one making the endowment must meet in order for the endowment to be considered valid. These are:

(1) The one making the endowment must be one legally capable of making donations. An endowment is not proper from one who has illegally seized property or who is

buying something and is not yet in full ownership of the thing that he wants to make an endowment.

(2) The one making the endowment must be sane. Endowments are not valid from the insane or weak of mind.

(3) The one making the endowment must be adult as endowments are not allowed from children, whether or not they have reached the "age of discernment".

(4) The one making the endowment must be someone who acts in a reasonable manner; endowments are not allowed from people who due to their stupidity or naiveté have been prohibited from dealing with their own wealth; nor are they allowed from the overly negligent.

Conditions for What is Being Made an Endowment

In order for the endowment to be executed, it must meet the following conditions:

(1) It must be wealth that has some value to it, either immovable property or otherwise.

(2) The endowment must be something known and specified.

(3) The endowment must be owned by the one making the endowment at the time he makes the endowment.

(4) The endowment must be privately owned and not commonly or publicly owned. It is not allowed to make one's share of public property an endowment.

(5) No one else may have any rights over the endowment.

(6) It must be the case that the benefit of the endowment is something commonly known.

(7) The benefits accruing from the endowment must be permissible.

How to Use the Benefits of Endowments

The benefits of endowments are obtained by their use, such as living in a house, riding an animal, using the wool, milk, eggs and fur of animals.

Topic Three:

The Difference Between an Endowment and a Bequest

There are a number of differences between an endowment and a bequest, including:

(1) In the case of an endowment, the property is maintained and not given away while the benefits or proceeds are given to others. In the case of a bequest, the ownership is attributed after the person's death to another by way of donation, regardless of whether it be the item itself or its usufruct.

(2) An endowment is binding and it is not allowed for a person to retract it according to the majority of the scholars. This is based on the statement of the Messenger of Allah (peace be upon him) to Umar,

إن شئت حبست أصلها وتصدقت بها

"If you wish, you may retain the property while giving [its proceeds] away in charity." Umar did so on the condition that its property would not be sold, given as a gift or inherited. [Recorded by al-Bukhari.] Umar gave the proceeds in charity to the poor, relatives, slaves buying their freedom, warriors fighting for the sake of Allah, travelers and visitors. There is no harm if the one in charge of it eats from it according to what is customarily acceptable or if he feeds a friend an amount which is not valuable.

As for an endowment, it is binding; however, it is permissible for the one making the bequest to rescind all or part of it.

(3) Endowment does not allow anyone to take over ownership of the endowed property; only the proceeds are owned. A bequest includes both the property itself and its proceeds.

(4) The ownership of the proceeds of an endowment becomes apparent during the lifetime of the one founding the endowment as well as after his death. The ownership of a bequest does not take effect until after the death of the one making the bequest.

(5) There is no limit to the maximum that one may give as an endowment. However, one may only bequeath up to one-third of one's property, unless the rightful heirs give their permission to give more.

(6) It is permissible to make one's heirs the benefactor of an endowment. In the case of a bequest, one may not bequeath anything to a rightful heir unless the other rightful heirs permit such an act.

Chapter Five: Bequests

This chapter comprises an introduction and a discussion of the following three topics:

Topic 1: Types of bequests and their legal status;
Topic 2: Conditions for a bequest;
Topic 3: What nullifies a bequest.

Introduction

Definition of a Bequest

A bequest is the command to perform some act or disposition after the death of the one making the bequest. It may include acts like fulfilling a trust, giving something in charity, marrying off one's daughters, washing the dead, praying upon him and so forth.

The Basis for the Legality of a Bequest

The basis for bequests is found in the Quran, sunnah and consensus. Allah says,

$$كُتِبَ عَلَيْكُمْ إِذَا حَضَرَ أَحَدَكُمُ الْمَوْتُ إِنْ تَرَكَ خَيْرًا الْوَصِيَّةُ$$

"It is prescribed, when death approaches any of you, if he leave any goods, that he make a bequest" (*al-Baqarah* 180). The Messenger of Allah (peace be upon him) said,

$$\text{مَا حَقُّ امْرِئٍ مُسْلِمٍ لَهُ شَيْءٌ يُوصِي فِيهِ يَبِيتُ لَيْلَتَيْنِ إِلاَّ وَوَصِيَّتُهُ مَكْتُوبَةٌ عِنْدَهُ}$$

"It is not right for any Muslim, when he has something that he wants to bequeath, to spend two nights except that his bequest is recorded with him." [Recorded by al-Bukhari.]

What Constitutes the Making of a Bequest

A bequest can be made in one of three ways: (1) by speech, (2) by recording or (3) by understood signaling.

(1) By speech: There is no disagreement among the jurists that a bequest can be made by explicit speech, such as a person saying, "I bequeath this to so and so." It can be done by implicit speech if it is understood by the context to refer to a bequest, such as, "I make such and such for so and so after my death," or, "Bear witness that I have bequeathed such and such to so and so."

(2) A bequest may be through writing if it is from a person who is mute and cannot speak.

(3) A bequest may also be made by understood signaling if the person is mute or is not able to speak for some reason. However, this is conditional upon the fact that the person is not able to speak.

Topic One:
The Types of Bequests and Its Legal Status

The Legal Status of a Bequest

A bequest is both legal and recommended, as Allah has said,

يَاأَيُّهَا الَّذِينَ آمَنُوا شَهَادَةُ بَيْنِكُمْ إِذَا حَضَرَ أَحَدَكُمُ الْمَوْتُ حِينَ الْوَصِيَّةِ اثْنَانِ ذَوَا عَدْلٍ مِنْكُمْ أَوْ آخَرَانِ مِنْ غَيْرِكُمْ إِنْ أَنْتُمْ ضَرَبْتُمْ فِي الْأَرْضِ فَأَصَابَتْكُمْ مُصِيبَةُ الْمَوْتِ

"O you who believe! When death approaches any of you, (take) witnesses among yourselves when making bequests, two just men of your own (brotherhood) or others from outside if you are journeying through the earth, and the chance of death befalls you" (*al-Maaidah* 102).

The Types of Bequests

(1) The obligatory bequest: This is a bequest upon a person who is in debt and who has some rights against him or some trusts or pacts that he must fulfill. It is obligatory upon him to make such matters clear by writing a definitive, explicit will that delineates the debt and states whether it is to be paid promptly or over time. It should also state what trusts or pacts he must fulfill so that the matter can be clear for his heirs when they take care of the dispositions that he has put them in charge of.

(3) The recommended and desirable bequests: This is wherein one bequests up to one-third of his wealth to persons

other than his rightful heirs. This [distribution] is recommended and can be given to charitable causes and other righteous outlets, regardless of whether it be to a specific relative, a non-relative or specific causes, such as a specific mosque, or general purposes, such as for the sake of mosques, schools, libraries, refugees, clinics and so on.

The Amount of a Bequest

It is not allowed for the bequest to be more than one-third of one's wealth. This point is based on the Prophet's statement to Saad when Saad said, "Can I give all of my wealth away in a bequest?" The Prophet (peace be upon him) replied, "No." He then asked, "How about one-half?" The Prophet (peace be upon him) said, "No." Then he said, "How about one-third?" He replied, "One-third [is permissible] but one-third is [still] much." (Recorded by al-Bukhari and Muslim.)

It is not permitted to make a bequest for a rightful heir or to make a bequest beyond one-third of one's wealth unless it is done by the permission of the other rightful heirs.

What is Taken Into Consideration for the Bequest to Be Valid

(1) It must be something fair and just.

(2) It must be in accord with what Allah has legislated through His Prophet (peace be upon him).

(3) The one making the bequest must do his deed purely for the sake of Allah and desire by his bequest the doing of righteous deeds and goodness.

Topic Two:

The Conditions of a Bequest

There are three factors or agents in a bequest: the one making the bequest, the one for whom the bequest is made and the object of the bequest. Each one of these has specific conditions that it must meet. The following notes the most important of such conditions:

Conditions for the One Making the Bequest

(1) He must be someone who is qualified to make donations.

(2) He must be the owner of the bequeathed property.

(3) He must make the bequest out of his own free will and choice.

Conditions for the One for Whom the Bequest is Made

(1) He must be a recipient for the sake of goodness or what is permissible.

(2) The one for whom the bequest is made must be existing, in reality or theoretically [such as a child in his mother's womb], at the time of the bequest. It is not valid to make a bequest for someone who does not exist.

(3) It must be a specified person.

(4) It must be one who has the legal capability to own.

(5) It cannot be the killer of the one making the bequest.

(6) It cannot be a legal heir.

Conditions for What is Being Bequeathed

(1) It must be wealth that could be inherited.

(2) The wealth bequeathed must be something of value according to Islamic law.

(3) It must be something that can be owned, even if it does not actually exist by the time the bequest is made.

(4) It must be part of the one making the bequest's property at the time of the bequest.

(5) What is bequeathed must not be sinful or forbidden according to Islamic law.

Confirming a Bequest

There is agreement that it is best to record the bequest, starting with the name of Allah, followed by praises to Allah and then prayers and blessings upon the Prophet (peace be upon him). Then the witnesses should make it known, either by writing or speech.

The Types of Executors

The executors may be one of three categories:

(1) A ruler

(2) A judge

(3) Any chosen one from among the Muslim individuals.

Topic Three:

Nullifiers of the Bequest

The following acts nullify the bequest:

(1) The person rescinds his bequest, either explicitly or by indication.

(2) The bequest was made conditional upon an act that did not occur.

(3) The thing that was bequeathed does not exist.

(4) The one making the bequest becomes no longer legally capable.

(5) According to some scholars, the one making the request apostatizes from Islam.

(6) The one for whom the bequest was made rejects the bequest.

(7) The one to specifically receive the bequest dies before the one making the bequest dies.

(8) The one for whom the bequest was made kills the one who made the bequest.

(9) The bequeathed property is destroyed or its rightful owners appear.

(10) The bequeath is voided if it is for a rightful heir and not approved by the other heirs.

Part Three:
Family Matters

This part shall be comprised of the following chapters:
Chapter One: Marriage and its rulings;
Chapter Two: Rulings particular for Muslim women.

Chapter One: Marriage and Its Rulings

This chapter is comprised of an introduction and a discussion of the following two topics:

Topic 1: Conditions and Legal Status of Marriage;

Topic 2: What is Recommended and What is Forbidden in Relation to Marriage.

Introduction

The Wisdom for Legalizing Marriage

Marriage is one of the established practices of Islam that was encouraged by the Messenger of Allah (peace be upon him). The Messenger of Allah (peace be upon him) said,

يَا مَعْشَرَ الشَّبَابِ مَنِ اسْتَطَاعَ الْبَاءَةَ فَلْيَتَزَوَّجْ فَإِنَّهُ أَغَضُّ لِلْبَصَرِ وَأَحْصَنُ لِلْفَرْجِ وَمَنْ لَمْ يَسْتَطِعْ فَعَلَيْهِ بِالصَّوْمِ فَإِنَّهُ لَهُ وِجَاءٌ

"O group of young people, whoever among you who has the ability to marry should get married. Certainly, it [helps] in lowering the gaze and keeps the private parts chaste. Whoever cannot [get married] should fast for it will be a protection for him." [Recorded, with this exact wording, by Muslim.]

The Wisdom Behind Marriage

Marriage is a sound setting leading to strong ties among families, reciprocal love, chastity and protection from forbidden acts.

Marriage is the best means to bring about children and increase the population while preserving proper lineage.

Marriage is from among the best means to satisfy the sexual urges and fulfill such needs while keeping such acts safe from disease.

Marriage satisfies the natural desire for fatherhood and motherhood which grows with the presence of children.

Marriage also leads to tranquillity, solace, modesty and chastity for the husband and wife.

Lexical and Legal Definition of Marriage

Lexically, the word *nikaah* (نِكَاح) means sexual intercourse or combining between two items and it is also commonly used to refer to the contract. One says, "*Nakaha* such and such a woman," if one is determined to marry her and fulfill the contract. If a person says, "*Nakaha* his wife," this means that he had sexual intercourse with her.

Legally, *nikaah* refers to the contract that has the explicit or clear mention of marriage and that brings about the right to enjoy one another, be spouses to each other and be companions for one another.

Topic One:
Conditions for Marriage and Its Legal Status

The Legal Status of Marriage

Marriage is a recommended act (sunnah) for anyone who has sexual desires but does not fear that he would actually go out and commit illegal sexual intercourse. Marriage becomes obligatory upon the one who has such a fear. It is permissible for one who does not have such desires, such as the impotent or aged. It is forbidden in *daar al-harb* [the lands at war with Islam] except in the case of necessity.

Its Verbal Form

Marriage is concluded by any word that clearly indicates it; that is, it can be in any language. For example, if one were to say, "I marry to you [so and so]," or, "I wed to you," and the other says, "I accept this marriage," or, "I marry her," or, "I am pleased by that," it would be an acceptable marriage contract. It is recommended to be in Arabic. Whoever does not know Arabic may state the offer and acceptance in his own language.

The Essential Components of a Marriage Contract

There are two essential components:
(1) The offer: This is the wording coming from the guardian or the one representing the guardian. It should be stated with proper forms of the word *nikaah* or *tazweej* for those who know Arabic. These words should be used because they are words in the Quran. For example, Allah says,

فَانكِحُوا مَا طَابَ لَكُمْ مِنَ النِّسَاءِ

"Marry women (*ankihoo*) of your choice" (*al-Nisaa* 3).

(2) The acceptance: This is the wording coming from the groom or his representative. It is by words such as, "I accept (*qabalt*) this marriage," or, "I am pleased with this marriage," or, simply, "I accept." The offer must come before the acceptance, unless the circumstances already point to it.

The Conditions for a Marriage Contract

In order for the marriage contract to be valid, the following four conditions must be met:

(1) The bride and the groom must be specified.

(2) Both the bride and the groom must be pleased by the marriage [that is, they are acceptable to one another]. It is not permissible to force either of them into marriage with the other. The permission of both the virgin and the non-virgin woman is sought. The permission of the virgin is her silence while the non-virgin states her approval. That is not required with respect to the insane or imbeciles.

(3) The guardian is also a condition. The guardian must be a free, adult, sane, rightly-guided, righteous Muslim who is of the same religion as the woman for whom he is a guardian. The father of the woman has the most right to be the guardian. Second would come his executor for marriage. Then comes her paternal grandfathers, no matter how far "up," such as great grandfather and so on. Next comes her sons, no matter how far "down," such as great grandson. Then comes her full brother, then her half brother through her father, then their sons, then her paternal uncles, then their sons, then her closest male relative from her father's side and then the ruler.

(4) Having witnesses is the fourth condition. A marriage is not valid without the presence of two, just, legally capable male witnesses.

Topic Two:
What is Recommended and What is Forbidden
with Regards to Marriage

It is recommended for a man to marry just one wife if he fears that he would not be just among more than one wife. He should choose a wife who is religious, not related to him, virgin, child-bearing and beautiful.

It is recommended for a man who wants to propose to a woman to take a look at her, what is other than her *aurah* (parts she must keep covered) and what would attract him to marry her, without being in private with her, so that the matter will be free of suspicion. The woman should also look at the one who is proposing to her.

If it is not possible for the man to see her, he may send a trustworthy woman to look at her and then describe her to him.

It is forbidden for a man to propose to a woman if another brother has already proposed to her [and his proposal was accepted], unless the other man gives up on that proposal.

It is forbidden to make an explicit statement of proposal to a woman who is fulfilling her mourning period and for the woman who is fulfilling her waiting period after her third divorce.[1] One, however, may make an indirect reference, such as, "I am desirous of marriage," and so forth.

It is permissible for the one who divorced a woman by an irrevocable divorce, but less than three times, to make her a direct or indirect proposal even while she is in her waiting period.

---

[1] When a man and woman are married to each other, they are allowed to divorce each other three times. After the third divorce, though, they cannot remarry until the woman marries another man, consummates her marriage with him and that marriage comes to an end.—JZ

It is forbidden to make either an explicit or indirect proposal to a divorced woman who is still going through her waiting period.

It is recommended to make the marriage contract in the late afternoon on Fridays, as that contains a time in which the supplications are responded to. It is also recommended to perform the contract in the mosque if that is feasible.

Chapter Two: Rulings Particular for Muslim Women

This chapter shall contain an introduction and a discussion of a number of issues.

Introduction

Since the address of the Lawgiver is addressed to those who are legally capable, such legislation is divided into three categories:
(1) That which is specifically for men.
(2) That which is specifically for women.
(3) That which is commonly directed to both men and women.

I would like to mention some of the most important fiqh rulings that are specifically related to women. Most of the fiqh rulings which are directed to both men and women have been discussed earlier.

Issues Specifically Related to Women

The First Issue: Wiping Over a Wig

It is permissible to wear a wig if there is some strong need to do so. If a woman needs to wear a wig, she does not wipe over it while making ablution for prayer. This is because it does not take on the same ruling or meaning as the headscarf. The woman must wipe directly over her head or over the hair which Allah has created.

The Second Issue: Fingernail or Toenail Polish

Some women apply fingernail or toenail polish and this completely covers the nail, preventing water from reaching to the skin or nail itself. This is not allowed. It can only be put on when one is in a state of purity and must be removed when one has to make a new ablution.[1]

The Third Issue: Menstruation

Menstruation refers to the blood that flows from the woman's vagina under normal, healthy circumstances which is not due to giving birth or deflowering. Many scholars are of the opinion that it may begin by the age of nine. If a girl sees blood before that age, it is not considered the menses but bleeding due to a disease or illness. It may continue until the end of a person's life. It usually stops by the time a woman reaches the age of fifty.

The blood that flows from the woman is of six color varieties: black, red, yellowish, dingy, greenish or muddy. [All of these will be considered her menses if they flow during her regular monthly cycle.]

The shortest time for an entire menses is one day and night. Its median is five days. The longest period is fifteen days. Normally, it is six or seven days.

---

[1] What the author means here is that while the woman is obliged to pray, she cannot make ablution while such nail polish is on because it prevents the water from reaching the parts that must be washed during the ablution.—JZ

The shortest time period for the time of purity between menses is usually thirteen days. It may actually be less or more than that.

While the woman is on her menses, it is forbidden for her to pray, fast, enter the mosque, recite the Quran from a copy of the Quran, circumambulate the Kaaba or have sexual intercourse. Menses are a sign that the woman has reached the age of puberty.

The Fourth Issue: Post-Partum Bleeding

Post-partum bleeding is the blood that flows from the woman's vagina after giving birth or when the greater portion of a child comes out, even if it is aborted but most of its physical being has become apparent.

This bleeding is usually for forty days. There is no specific minimum time period for it. If a woman gives birth to twins, the period of post-partum bleeding begins with the birth of the first child, not the second.

The same things that are forbidden for a menstruating woman are also forbidden for a woman with post-partum bleeding, such as prayer, fasting and so forth.

The Fifth Issue: *al-Istahaadhah* (Abnormal Prolonged Flow of Blood)

Al-Istahaadhah (الاستحاضة) refers to a flow of blood from the vagina that is not during the time of the menses or post-partum bleeding. It also includes any blood that flows beyond the maximum period of the menses or post-partum bleeding as well as what flows for less than the minimum time of the menses. It also includes any blood that flows before the age of puberty, which is nine years of age.

The ruling concerning *istihaadhah* is that it is a continuous state that does not prevent one from performing the prayer or fasting. The woman suffering from this condition should make ablution for every prayer. It is permissible for her to have sexual intercourse with her husband. The blood that a pregnant woman sees during her pregnancy is also considered blood of *istihaadhah*.

The Sixth Issue: Shaving Hair and Other Issues

It is prohibited for women to shave their hair [from their heads] unless due to some strong need. It is also forbidden for her to remove or lessen the hairs from her eyebrows, be tattooed, add hair to her own or make a space between her teeth. The Messenger of Allah (peace be upon him) cursed the one who performed these acts and the one to whom they were performed, as recorded by al-Bukhari, Muslim, Abu Dawood, al-Nasaai, al-Tirmidhi, ibn Maajah and Ahmad.

It is forbidden for a woman to wear perfume except for her husband or while among only women.

The Seventh Issue: The *Aurah* of a Woman

[The *aurah* refers to the "private parts" of a person, in the sense that this is what a person must cover in front of others under different circumstances.] All of the woman is considered *aurah* when she is in the presence of men other than those men who are so closely related to her that she cannot marry them. Hence, she must cover all of herself in front of such men. Furthermore, it is not allowed for her to be in complete privacy with such men.

It is not allowed for a woman to travel except in the company of men to whom she is closely related. Those are the men whom she can never marry due to a permissible relationship between them of either blood, marriage or breastfeeding.

In prayer, the woman must cover all of her body save her face, hands and feet. However, she must also cover all of those parts of her body if she is praying in the presence of men she is not closely related to. Furthermore, it is recommended for her to cover her hands and feet under all circumstances.

The clothes covering the body must be loose and thick [not see-through] and must not resemble men's clothing. They also must not have designs on them such that they attract the looks of people. They also should not resemble the clothing of the disbelievers nor can they be clothes of show and ostentation.

The Eighth Issue: Beautification for Women

Some articles of beautification are permissible for women while others are forbidden. They are permitted to use perfume, gold, silver, silk and saffron dyed clothing. It is forbidden for them to use articles of beautification that are meant for showing off or being ostentatious or that turn people's looks to them. They are also not allowed to wear perfume that has a fragrance and then go out amidst men to whom they are not closely related.

The Ninth Issue: The Voice of Women

The voice of a woman is not *aurah* [does not need to be concealed] unless she tries to make it soft and alluring to men. It is forbidden for her to sing. Unfortunately, nowadays many are madly in love with singing and have used it as a way to attract others and earn money. Singing is forbidden for men and it is even more so forbidden for women. It is permissible for women only on special occasions of happiness and on Eids, and that only while among other women and with songs that have praiseworthy meanings to them and without any musical accompaniment to them.

The Tenth Issue: Related to Death and Funerals

It is permissible for a woman to wash her young child or her husband [after their death]. It is also permissible for her to perform the funeral prayer, just like men. However, it is not permissible for her to follow the funeral procession and escort it to the burial site. It is also not allowed for her to visit the gravesites. She is forbidden to wail, lament, slap her cheeks, tear her clothing or to rip her hair out. All of those deeds are from the practices of the days of Ignorance and constitute great sins. It is not allowed for a woman to mourn for anyone other than her husband for more than three days. With respect to her husband, she mourns for four months and ten days. During that time, she must stay in the house of her husband and refrain from any types of adornment or perfume. However, there is no specific clothing that she wears for mourning.

The Eleventh Issue: Jewelry

A woman is free to wear what Allah has permitted her of gold and silver jewelry, according to what is customary and acceptable. She must avoid extravagance and arrogance. She does not have to pay zakat on her gold or silver jewelry as long as she wears it regularly or on special occasions.

The Twelfth Issue: Women Giving Charity

It is permissible for a woman to give in charity from her husband's wealth without his permission as long as it is something customary and she knows that he would be pleased with it. She may give the zakaat on her wealth to him if he is from the recipients of zakaat. If her husband is stingy and does not spend on his family what is obligatory upon him, then she, without his permission, may take a fair amount from his wealth for herself and her children.

The Thirteenth Issue: Breaking the Fast

A pregnant or breastfeeding woman may break her fast if she fears any harm for herself alone or for both herself and her child. In those cases, she simply has to make up those days later without any kind of penalty or "ransom". But if the pregnant woman fears not for herself but only for her child, then she must make up the day later as well as fulfill the penalty. As for the breastfeeding woman, if the child accepts another woman's breast and the mother has the ability to pay that woman, then she should hire that woman to breastfeed her child and she does not break her fast. The ruling concerning the hired breastfeeding woman is the same as the ruling for the mother concerning the above [matters of fearing only for herself or for both herself and the child].

It is not permissible for a woman to perform a voluntary fast without the permission of her husband if he is present.

The Fourteenth Issue: Performing the Pilgrimage

The husband is not allowed to prevent his wife from performing her obligatory pilgrimage. If she asks him for permission, he must permit her and help her by facilitating the performance of the pilgrimage that Allah has made obligatory upon her. As for a voluntary pilgrimage, he may prevent her from doing such if it causes any kind of hardship for himself or her children.

The Fifteenth Issue: Clothing During the Pilgrimage

A woman can wear her customary clothing during the pilgrimage but she must refrain from the following: (1) clothing that is perfumed, (2) gloves, (3) face veil and (4) clothing dyed with saffron.

The Sixteenth Issue: Pilgrimage During Menses and Post-Partum Bleeding

Women on their menses or with post-partum bleeding perform the *ghusl*, enter the inviolable state and perform all of the rites of the pilgrimage except for circumambulating the House. They do not circumambulate the House until they become pure from their state.

The Seventeenth Issue: The *Talbiyyah*

The pilgrims should chant the *talbiyyah*.[1] The men should raise their voices while the women say it quietly. Furthermore, women do not follow the practice of trotting during the circumambulation or the *sa'ee*. They also do not raise their voices while supplicating, nor do they crowd in to get to the black stone or other locations.

The Eighteenth Issue: Cutting the Hair as a Rite of Pilgrimage

Cutting or shaving the hair is one of the rites of the pilgrimage and the umrah. For the woman, cutting the hair

---

[1] This is the saying of, *"Labaika-llahumma labaik labaika laa shareeka laka labaik. Inna-l-hamda wa-nimata laka wa-l-mulk. Laa shareeka lak* (O Allah, here I am at your service. You have no partner. Here I am at your service. Verily, all the praise and the grace belong to You, and the Dominion [as well]. You have no partner)."

takes the place of shaving the hair, since it is not allowed for a woman to shave her hair. The manner in which a woman cuts her hair for this rite is to cut off a fingertip's worth from every braid or she gathers her hair together, if it is not in braids, and cuts off that amount from it.

The Nineteenth Issue: The Farewell Circumambulation

It is preferred for the women to perform the circumambulation of returning from Mina early on the Day of Sacrifice if they fear that their menses are coming. Aishah would tell the women to perform that circumambulation early on the Day of Sacrifice out of fear that they may experience their menses. If a woman is menstruating, she does not have to perform the farewell circumambulation if she had already performed the circumambulation after returning from Mina and if her departure time is while she is on her menses.

The Twentieth Issue: Marrying Non-Muslims

It is not allowed for a Muslim woman to marry a non-Muslim, regardless of whether he be a polytheist— socialist, Hindu or other— or from the People of the Book. This is because the man has the right of heading the household over his wife and she must obey him. This is the meaning of such authority. It is not proper for a disbeliever or polytheist to have any kind of authority or rule over any one who bears witness that there is none worthy of worship except Allah and that Muhammad (peace be upon him) is the Messenger of Allah.

The Twenty-First Issue: Custody

Custody refers to taking care of a small male or female child or an incompetent person. The mother has the right to have custody over the male or female child. She is forced to do so if she refuses. After her, in this right, comes her mother, then the mother's mother and then her mother and so on, and then comes the father and then his mother, then the grandfather, then his mother, then the full sister, then the half-sister through the mother, then the half-sister through the father, then the mother's sisters, then the father's sisters, then the father's sisters of her mother, then the father's maternal aunts, then the mother's father's maternal aunts, then her nieces from her sisters, then her cousins from her mother's side, then her cousins from her father's side and so forth. It continues in this manner until, if there are no more such relatives, the ruler takes charge of the child.

The father must pay the wages of the one who has the custody. In order to qualify for such custody, the person must be adult, sane, able to bring up the child, trustworthy, of good character, Muslim and not married. If the mother gets remarried, she loses her right to custody. If a boy reaches the age of seven, he is free to choose which parent he wishes to stay with. After the age of seven, the father has more right to his daughter until he gives her over to her husband.

The Twenty-Second Issue: Covering the Face

The scholars of the four schools of fiqh, even those among them who say that the face and hands are not part of the *aurah*, are in agreement that it is obligatory upon the woman to cover all of her body in the presence of non-related men—those who say that such is not part of the *aurah* say that during immoral times, times of little piety and times in which men look often at women, like what is occurring today, women are required to cover their faces and hands.

      This is what I have been able to compile and collect in this short span of time. I ask the Lord and Guardian, the Exalted, the Powerful to make this work beneficial. Allah is behind every intention and He is the guide to the straight path.

      This was completed at the beginning at Dhu-l-Hijjah, 1413 A.H.

AL-BASHEER BOOK TITLES

Commentary on the Forty Hadith of Al-Nawawi {Vol. 1-3} –
Jamaal Zarabozo   80.00

Fiqh Made Easy – Saalih Al-Sadlaan   11.00

He Came to Teach You Your Religion – Jamaal Zarabozo   11.00

How to Approach & Understand the Quran –
Jamaal Zarabozo   16.00

Marital Discord 'Al-Nushooz' – Saalih Sadlaan   6.00

Purification of the Soul – Jamaal Zarabozo   29.00

Religious Extremism - Abdul-
Rahman ibn Mualaa al-Luwaihiq al-Mutairi   35.00

The Authority and Importance of the Sunnah –
Jamaal Zarabozo   16.00

*The Fiqh of Marriage in the Light of the Quraan
and Sunnah* – Saalih Al-Sadlaan   10.00

Congregational Prayer – Saalih Al-Sadlaan   15.00

The World of the Jinn and Devils – Jamaal Zarabozo   11.00

Towards Understanding Our Religion – Jamaal Zarabozo   17.00

Words of Remembrance and Words of Reminder
w/ audio CD – Saalih Al-Sadlaan   9.00

AL-BASHEER CD & DVD TITLES

Lives of the Prophets Vol 1 & 2
(Anwar Al-Awlaki 9 CDs) 35.00

Lives of the Prophets Volumes 3 & 4
(Anwar Al- Awlaki 12 CDs) 45.00

Lives of the Prophets Vols 1-4 Complete Set
(21 CDs Anwar Al-Awlaki) 80.00

The Hereafter Volume 1
(10 Cds by Anwar Al-Awlaki) 35.00

The Hereafter: Volume 2
(Set of 12 CDs) by Anwar Al-Awlaki 35.00

The Hereafter-Vol 1 & 2 Complete Set
(22 CDs Anwar Al-Awlaki) 80.00

2in1 - The Hereafter & Lives Of The Prophets
(Complete Set of 43 CDs Anwar Al-Awlaki) 150.00

Abu Bakr al Siddiq: His Life and Times
(Set of 15 CDs) by Anwar Al-Awlaki 55.00

Ummar Ibn Alkhataab: His Life And Times
(Set of 18 CDs Anwar Al-Awlaki) 65.00

2in1-Abu Bakr Al Siddiq & Ummar Ibn Alkhataab
(Set of 33 CDs Anwar Al-Awlaki) 110.00

4 sets - The Hereafter, Lives Of The Prophets, Ummar Ibn
Alkhataab & Abu Bakr Al Siddiq
(76 CDs by Anwar Al-Awlaki) 250.00

The Last Juz- Qur'an in North America
(Single CD by Imam Sayed Jomaa) 5.00

Envy (Hasad) -a disease that affects many hearts
(Set of 7 CDs by Jamaal Zarabozo) 35.00

A Guide For The New Muslim
(Set of 12 CDs by Jamaal Zarabozo) 44.95

Youth Matters: Extremism -
A Discussion Long Overdue (DVD by Raeed Tayeh) 12.95